A Political Reading of the
Life of Jesus

A Political Reading of the Life of Jesus

George W. Baldwin

Robin —

MFSA 100th

George W. Baldwin

iUniverse, Inc.
New York Lincoln Shanghai

A Political Reading of the Life of Jesus

iUniverse books may be ordered through booksellers or by contacting:

iUniverse
2021 Pine Lake Road, Suite 100
Lincoln, NE 68512
www.iuniverse.com
1-800-Authors (1-800-288-4677)

ISBN-13: 978-0-595-41579-3 (pbk)
ISBN-13: 978-0-595-85927-6 (ebk)
ISBN-10: 0-595-41579-2 (pbk)
ISBN-10: 0-595-85927-5 (ebk)

Printed in the United States of America

Contents

Foreword by Fr. Miguel d'Escoto

Thank you for giving me the privilege of reading your book: *A Political Reading of the Life of Jesus.*

Yours has been a wonderful Spirit-filled faith adventure. In it, because He loves you so much and because you allowed yourself to be guided by Him, He revealed more of His mystery to you than to most people.

From the very start of your book I could feel my heart beating with the kind of joy that one often experiences in those special moments when His presence seems so real. I felt totally one with you when you moved towards a radical, biblical and dangerous understanding of God.

I could not agree more with you in saying that "we need to recover the Jesus who challenged the powers with non-violent *agape*." And yes, by all means, to accept to follow Jesus means to choose, in obedience to Him, to engage in the Politics of Liberation and Freedom.

I also am very much with you when you say that "to accept the idea of a 'just war' is to adopt the mind of the oppressor," and this approach to the struggle for freedom only perpetuates the cycle of violence and serves the interest of Power.

My hope and only real purpose in these last few years has been to deepen the understanding (mine as well as others) of this great truth that you so humbly and Christ-like have expressed so well. I feel the great need of a re-insurrection.

Your brother,

Miguel d'Escoto

Maryknoll Priest and Foreign Minister for Nicaragua from 1979–1990

Acknowledgments

I would like to thank my parents, Kenneth and Florence Baldwin, who gave me a good grounding in Montana Methodism. I am indebted to all the members of churches I served as a pastor for twelve years. I am grateful for the fourteen stimulating years I was on the faculty at Saint Paul School of Theology (United Methodist) in Kansas City, Missouri

The people (*el pueblo*) of Nicaragua are the source of inspiration for this book. I was privileged to share in their daily lives, in the Christian Base Communities (*Las Comunidades de Base*), and as a participant in *La Insurrección Evangelica* (The Gospel Insurrection). Of the many in Nicaragua I must lift up three persons: Jaime Feltz, Montserrat Fernandez, and Fr. Miguel d'Escoto,

Many persons have contributed to this book through their suggestions to improve the manuscript and by their ongoing encouragement: Rev. James Uhlig, Dorothy Eck, Bob Roughton, Bill and Fran McElvaney, Rev. LaVerne Sugamele and her husband Jerry Sugamele. Dr. Bob Holmes and his wife Polly Holmes both died before they could see the fruits of our mutual endeavor to be persons of faith through the publication of this book.

Finally, I dedicate this book to my four children: Cindy, Kevin, Kathy and Mark.

Introduction

○ ○

"Enter through the narrow gate: for the gate is wide and the road is easy that leads to destruction, and there are many who take it. For the gate is narrow and the road is hard that leads to life, and there are few who find it."

—Jesus

For over 2000 years Christendom has made the life and teachings of Jesus irrelevant in the realm of politics. Rather than being a threat to those who operate from positions of power and manifest the desire to dominate, Jesus has been domesticated by being relegated to the realm of religion and thusly placed in servitude to those in Power.

This book is an attempt to explore the political significance of Jesus' life and to reflect upon how it relates to our contemporary life. Jesus provides a compelling model for political action. Indeed, a thoughtful examination of Jesus' life and teachings reveals the proper integration of politics and religion.

Any objective reading of the New Testament will disclose two powerful themes to be found in the Christian Bible: 1) The Biblical theme of Salvation and 2) The Biblical theme of Liberation. A cursory reading of Church History will reveal that the theme of "salvation" has been the common expression of Christianity, and as such, represents no serious influence upon or threat to the Powers. However, a clear understanding of the theme of "liberation," has not been promoted in Western Civilization because it represents a challenge to the injustices which accompany the systems of domination. It is my hope that by reflecting upon the conflicts and tensions that exist between these two powerful Biblical themes that the reader will identify the social/political dimensions of his or her faith journey, as well as a more intense meaning in matters of personal integrity.

Freedom of religion is one of the basic political concepts we enjoy in the United States of America. The separation of Church and State, which is written in the Constitution, is the guiding principle for safeguarding freedom of religion.

This primarily means that the State cannot legislate a particular set of religious doctrines or an understanding of God (theology) to which every citizen must submit. The Constitution supports the right of each citizen to formulate his or her own Credo or statement of belief about God. For that matter, each citizen is granted the Constitutional right to be an atheist or a non-believer. Regrettably, for the great majority of our citizens, freedom "of" religion has meant freedom "from" doing their theological homework. Generally speaking people have not developed a clear theology and/or other foundational beliefs with which to address the awesome challenges which life presents.

The separation of Church and State is currently being threatened in at least two ways:

First: The separation of Church and State is often confused with the separation of *politics* and *religion*. The erroneous notion that there should be the separation of politics and religion often comes from the perception that religion is not essential for addressing the harder issues of life, which are supposedly dealt with in the realm of politics and government. This mistaken tendency serves the interests of the Powers and systems of domination to the detriment of the individual citizen.

Second: Current alliances between some political and religious leaders represent strategic attempts to impose matters of doctrine and morality upon other citizens through legislation at both the Federal and State levels. We need only to reflect on the process of the 2004 national and state elections to see that these represent a very real threat to the separation of Church and State. This self-serving promotion of imposed religious doctrine on the whole society also works in the interests of the Powers and systems of domination to the detriment of the individual citizen.

Some Christians attempt to resolve current personal and social issues by asking, "What would Jesus do?" However, approaching life's issues from the theme of "salvation" lends itself to little serious action. A more comprehensive approach asks the question, "What did Jesus do?" It is in response to this question that the theme of "liberation" comes alive as we see how Jesus' heart and soul was focused on matters of justice and freedom. He did not offer abstract instructions about how to challenge the Powers and domination systems of his day; he just did it. For any person who wants to take Jesus seriously, his example becomes our model.

From the very beginning of Ronald Reagan's presidency in 1980, his Administration was waging a covert, secret war against the Sandinista Revolution in Nicaragua. U.S. citizens became more aware of the Contra war in Nicaragua a few years later when the Iran-Contra Affair revealed the immoral and illegal actions of the U. S. foreign policy against this small Central American nation.

After several years of reflection and discernment, it was on the occasion of my 50th birthday (October 1983) that I came to the firm belief that God was calling me to participate fully with those who live in poverty. I resigned from my position as a professor at a United Methodist seminary, where I had been teaching for 14 years. I also returned my credentials to the United Methodist Church. I divested myself of my worldly goods and in the fall of 1984 I went to live in Nicaragua as an independent person.

In the Central Region of Nicaragua there were thousands of persons living in abject poverty as a result of being displaced from their homes and farms by the U. S. supported Contras who operated from a strategy of terrorism and violence. Shortly after the beginning of the 1985 I joined a Catholic Priest and his co-workers as they endeavored to participate with victims who were stranded in the middle of a war-zone. To rebuild their lives and survive the violence was no small challenge. By sharing my life with these courageous and faithful people deep within the jungles of Nicaragua I learned firsthand about the importance of the Biblical theme of "Liberation." Indeed, reading the story of Jesus through the eyes of those who are oppressed and live in the context of poverty opened me to new levels of awareness and changed my Credo.

Bill Moyers, a respected television journalist, identified a split in the United Methodist Church in terms of how its members viewed the situation in Nicaragua and whether or not to send missionaries to Nicaragua. Some United Methodist churches were withholding funds that would be used for that purpose. Conflicting views about the war were also being experienced within other church denominations as well as the public at large. Moyers decided to make a documentary on the subject.

Bill Moyers put his own life at risk as he traveled into this "war zone" for a face-to-face interview with me. As the interview progressed and matters of faith and politics were discussed, the following exchange occurred:

- **<u>Bill Moyers</u>**: "You're a dangerous man, you know that."

- <u>George Baldwin</u>: "I don't know that *(embarrassed, chuckle)*."

- **<u>Bill Moyers</u>**: "If your example were followed, multiplied, your ideas spread, they are subversive to the world."

- <u>George Baldwin</u>, "I like the way you put that. They *(my ideas)* are subversive to the world if we conceive of the world as a world defined by the

Powers that currently are in control. That's right; I do want to be a danger to that world."

♦   ♦   ♦

(Subsequently, on December 7, 1987, Moyer's documentary, *God and Politics: The Kingdom Divided*, was broadcast on Public Affairs Television in the United States.)

♦   ♦   ♦

Jesus' admonition to enter **The Narrow Gate** is still relevant.

Proceed with caution because Jesus calls for a far more radical commitment than most of us are ready to make.

This is my Credo!

PART I

A Political Reading of the Life of Jesus

1

The Politics of Jesus

Jesus knew his history. He profoundly understood the cycles of victory and defeat his Jewish homeland had experienced during previous centuries. At the time of his birth, and throughout his life, his nation suffered from an oppressive occupation by the Roman Empire.

Jesus was an astute political analyst. He could easily sympathize with the yearning of his contemporaries for a "Savior" or "Liberator" to lead them to freedom. Such a "Christ" or "Messiah" would not only achieve a military victory over the Roman oppressors but restore Israel to the political prominence it once enjoyed in that region during the reigns of King David and King Solomon.

Jesus recognized that the armed insurrection being promoted by many of his contemporaries would only result in another cycle of violence and end in disaster. It was clear to him that the Roman Empire would not tolerate such an uprising.

After Jesus died *that is exactly what happened!*

In the year AD66 a violent Jewish insurrection against Roman authority was led by a group called Zealots. Nero, the Roman Emperor, sent a general named Vespasian to put an end to the uprising. By the year AD70 the rebellion had been crushed, the Jewish Temple knocked down and the Holy City of Jerusalem devastated.

If the people had listened to Jesus this great disaster might never have happened.

Trying to discern Jesus' approach to the struggle for the liberation and freedom of his people is relevant to the struggle against the Powers and domination systems of today. Below: I summarize what I perceive to be Jesus' model for political activism and the way it clashes with the political model utilized by oppressive systems both then and now.

The Political Model of Jesus	*VS.*	*The Political Model of the Powers*
The Politics of Liberation and Freedom	**vs.**	The Politics of Power and Domination
A Theology of Grace	**vs**.	A Theology of Law and Judgment
A Methodology of Non-Violent Agape	**vs.**	A Methodology of Violence

The Political Model of Jesus

The Politics of Liberation and Freedom

Jesus was undeniably engaged in the political arena as he introduced the Politics of Liberation and Freedom. A careful reading of the Gospels shows that Jesus spoke of the Kingdom of God more than anything else. His message was understood by his listeners as a political agenda. Jesus believed that God was a full participant in the cycles of political oppression and liberation that had shaped the history of the Jewish People. Once again his nation was under the occupation of a foreign power.

The politics of liberation and freedom is about the pursuit of justice and not simply victory over the enemy. Beyond the need to avoid a violent insurrection that would inevitably lead to a major catastrophe for his homeland, Jesus was promoting the cause of universal human freedom.

Jesus drew his vision of liberation and the pursuit of justice from the scriptures whose stories he had learned as a child. As was the case with the Prophets, Jesus could see that to achieve freedom for his homeland he must confront the systemic evil which was deeply rooted in the religious systems and governance structures of his own nation as well as those imposed by the Roman Empire.

Jesus' goal was not to bring about a change of regimes from one political ideology to a new regime that would embrace the same methods required to maintain domination through power and violence. The Kingdom of God, as both an expression of theology and as a political ideology involved the creation of new social structures based on the love of neighbor.

Jesus rejected the role of a Messiah who would attempt to achieve a military victory. His vision of how to achieve freedom entailed a commitment of love, faith and passion from each person. To follow Jesus and engage in the politics of liberation and freedom meant to put one's life at risk. Jesus had no doubts that God would be a full participant with the people in their pursuit of freedom and justice.

For Jesus to succeed in promoting the Kingdom of God he would need to win the hearts and minds of the people. Freedom would not happen as a quick fix or miracle. Systemic change entails a long view of the struggle. It would require undaunted courage to engage in an uprising against the Roman occupation. The Roman Army was a well trained military force, which was known for its brutality. Those who engage in active resistance against the Powers and domination systems must be ready to pay the price.

Rather than a direct confrontation with the Roman authorities Jesus directed most of his challenges at the religious and political leaders of his own nation who were cooperating with the Roman authorities. For instance, by eating grain or healing on the Sabbath, which was prohibited, Jesus and his followers were not simply engaging in personal rebellion against religious dogma, but were challenging the very structures of political control.

Jesus understood that active political resistance to systemic injustice would result in disrupting the status quo of the Jewish establishment and ultimately lead to an encounter with Pontius Pilate, the Roman Governor, who ruled with a heavy hand. Jesus saw how the Romans dealt with political prisoners. Crucifixion was the method of choice to deter political uprisings. Even still, Jesus continued in his pursuit of freedom and invited others to believe that love, God's love, is a stronger force than fear or violence.

A Theology of Grace

The foundation upon which Jesus based both his politics and his spirituality was a Theology of Grace. Through both his actions and his words Jesus revealed his understanding of God. For Jesus, grace meant to trust in a God with whom one can have a relationship; a God who accepts people with an unconditional love; a God who is a full participant in human affairs; a God who is dedicated to bringing about freedom and justice.

In our English language we use the word "love" in various ways and with different meanings depending on the situation. Therefore, we must use a number of different descriptive adjectives to designate how we are using the word. In the New Testament, which was written in the Greek language, three separate words are used to express "love." *Eros* relates to the emotional or erotic nature of love. *Philia* is in reference to the expression of brotherly love or the love between friends. *Agape* is used to describe the nature of God's love

Also, in the English language, we use the word "love" as both a noun and a verb. The same is true for the word "*agape*." Throughout this book I will refer to *agape* as the kind of fervent good will and burning passion needed to achieve true freedom and to address injustice and evil in all of their various forms.

Grace negates the idea that we can earn or assume that in some way we deserve God's love. In his attempt to win the hearts and minds of his people, Jesus invited persons to experience God's freely given, undeserved *agape* and then to become the bearers of God's *agape* to others. Both the personal and social dimensions of Jesus' life were shaped by the fundamental understanding that God is the source of *agape*. Grace goes beyond the matter of personal religious experience to the context of socio/political action.

For Jesus, grace begins with God and is the foundation which leads to justice and freedom.

A Methodology of Non-violent Agape

In the story of the Exodus when God delivered the Hebrew people from bondage in Egypt it would appear that God engaged in acts of violence to achieve some objectives. In keeping with that tradition of violence, political insurgents, known as Zealots, were actively promoting a violent uprising against Roman authority.

However, because Jesus understood that engaging in violence never succeeds in delivering the peace that is promised, he was organizing an alternative model for insurrection based on an entirely different understanding of God and a radically different method for struggle. Jesus intended to break the cycle of violence which had plagued the history of his people by using a Methodology of Non-violent Agape.

Jesus' understanding of God was seen as blasphemy by the religious authorities. Engaging in the method of non-violent *agape* was met with violence on the part of the Jewish establishment. Indeed, it quickly brought forth enough rage for the High Priests to initiate serious plots designed to see Jesus killed.

In the Middle-Eastern Hebrew culture in which Jesus was reared, politics and religion were always integrated. They were interwoven to the point that for both Jesus and his cousin, John, there was no separation of religion and politics. To address either subject always engaged both dimensions of their lives.

John prepared the way for the insurrection. John had been preaching a message of repentance. He was inviting the people to repent (turn around) from their willingness to cooperate with the injustice which had become the norm for the leaders of his Jewish nation. John called for the people to turn back to God and commit themselves to seek justice. The sign of repentance was to submit to the ritual of cleansing, referred to as baptism. Thus he became known as "John the Baptist."

John believed that it was Jesus and not himself who would ultimately lead the way to attain freedom for their homeland. When Jesus was baptized it was a demonstration of his participation with the pain and suffering of his people and his willingness to challenge the Powers of this world. However, as it turned out, John was the first martyr in the political insurrection that ultimately led Jesus to the cross.

In the Gospels there is a story about a lawyer who, intending to test him, asked Jesus a question, "Teacher, which commandment in the law is the greatest?" Jesus answered, "You shall *agape (love)* the Lord your God with all your heart, and with all your soul and with all your mind." "This," Jesus said, "is the greatest and first commandment." Jesus went on to say, that a second commandment is like it: "You shall *agape* your neighbor as yourself." Jesus kept it clear and simple. In plain talk he was saying that if these two basic actions were undertaken, the rest would fall in place.

It is not easy for those of us who live in the Western culture to keep in mind that this response to the lawyer was a political statement as well as a religious statement. We must read the Bible with a new level of critical consciousness in order to recognize that *these two guiding principles represent the proper integration of politics and religion.*

Jesus underscored the spiritual dimensions of political struggle by teaching that *agape* was needed to achieve freedom and justice in this world. Jesus taught *agape* of God, *agape* of neighbor, *agape* of self and perhaps most important of all, *agape* for one's enemies. On more than one occasion he said there was no greater expression of *agape* than to lay down one's life for one's friends. Although non-violent *agape* seemed an impossible way to achieve the goal of liberation and freedom, Jesus held true to his own belief that all things were possible with God.

Jesus began his struggle for national liberation in the countryside. Initially he avoided any confrontation in Jerusalem, which was the socio/political center of his nation. His reputation for healing and teaching always had political implications in the promotion of the Kingdom of God. A non-violent populist movement was set in motion and grew as Jesus' reputation spread.

Jesus did not deceive the people with regard to the cost of engaging in a struggle for liberation and freedom. He said, "If any want to become my followers, let them deny themselves and take up their cross and follow me." There was no confusion in this invitation. The people, like Jesus, had seen crosses on which political prisoners had been crucified. Even in the face of this threat of state-sponsored terrorism Jesus was openly inviting people to participate in a political uprising.

There is no way to miss the point. By undertaking the politics of liberation and freedom Jesus was inviting people to be part of an insurrection, which may even cost them their lives. He was not asking them to do something that he was unwilling to do himself. Jesus knew that going to Jerusalem would more than likely result in his death. His closest comrades appealed to him not to go.

When the time was right to engage in direct action Jesus went to Jerusalem. As Jerusalem came into view Jesus wept, and said, "If you had only recognized on this day the things that make for peace! But now they are hidden from your eyes."

Jesus' promotion of The Politics of Liberation and Freedom, The Theology of Grace and The Methodology of Non-violent Love seemed to have fallen on deaf ears. Even his closest comrades were not ready to take up the cross.

After Jesus was arrested the people were given a choice by Pilate about which prisoner to release. They were given a choice between Jesus and Barrabas, who was also a political prisoner and not just an ordinary criminal. Under the influence of the Jewish High Priests and due to their own failure to understand Jesus, the people held to their vision of a military victory by calling for the release of Barrabas.

Make no mistake; because Jesus was challenging the "status quo" of his day, he was killed as a political prisoner. To miss the political implications of what Jesus was doing is to miss the point of his life in this world.

When Jesus was crucified it appeared that he had failed in his attempt to win the hearts and minds of the people. The non-violent insurrection he tried to set in motion did not save Jerusalem from destruction. Still, as we shall see, there is more to the story

The Political Model of the Powers

The Politics of Power and Domination

Jesus was challenging political and religious authorities who operated from the Politics of Power and Domination. Over the course of history this model has changed very little. It continues to be the basic model for political involvement embraced by those who govern and exercise power in the so-called "civilized world" of today.

Nation states, corporations, military organizations, educational institutions, legal systems, labor unions, self interest groups and even family structures may be identified as systems that utilize power over others as their mode of operation.

The institutional church in its various forms and structures is no exception. Throughout the book I will be referring to these systems as the *Powers*.

Competition is fierce within and between systems that operate from this model of political endeavor. Political strategies are calculated to maintain supremacy over any other forces that would dispute or defy their authority. The fear of losing control is a constant concern. Therefore, the Powers must be constantly vigilant to address any threats they perceive whether they are authentic or imagined. We may have a better insight into how this approach to politics functions if we think of it as the "politics of fear."

While the Powers speak publicly about lofty goals of freedom and democracy, their true motivation is to dominate. In spite of the rhetoric and public relations promotions the Powers are not concerned with creating social structures that offer true justice. For instance, a cursory examination of our legal system illustrates that for the most part, it is designed to benefit the rich and powerful and not the poor and disenfranchised.

The domination of people within a culture is accomplished early in life through the teaching of values and social customs which benefit those in power. Such values are embedded in our day to day lives, indeed, in our very being. Paulo Freire, a Brazilian educator and theologian of the last century, refers to this as "the mind of the oppressor." Freire made it clear that effective involvement in the political process requires the development of "critical consciousness" as persons begin to recognize their power as subjects who engage in changing their world as opposed to being acted upon. Offering resistance is at the heart of the battle for "hearts and minds."

For instance, the notion of "patriotism," based on a demand for total allegiance to the nation state, supports the policies of those in power. When the policies of those in authority are challenged, the accusation of being "un-patriotic" may be enough to deter people from further challenges. If not, they risk being subjected to more social ostracism or abuse not only by the Powers, but by their friends and neighbors who continue to operate from the "mind of the oppressor.

The Powers promote the illusion that we are at peace when the systems of domination are not being challenged. Those who seek freedom from injustice inevitably disturb the status-quo and are accused of being the cause of any violence that comes from the conflict. Jesus understood the deception hidden in the promise that peace can be achieved through violence. Oppressive domination may result in the absence of hostilities for a period of time, but it will never bring about true peace. Jesus understood that even though the challenge to those in authority is done in the form of non-violent resistance, the forthcoming response will be one of violence. Violence always accompanies domination which is why it is necessary to have a long view of the struggle.

A Theology of Law and Judgment

A theology of law and judgment provides the religious foundation that supports the politics of power and domination. In response to any challenge to their authority the Powers believe they have the moral right and duty, "*under God*," to take whatever measures are required to maintain control.

This kind of theology was manifest in the erroneous concept of the "divine right of kings." Sadly, this sense of entitlement to exercise power over others continues to be expressed by many who hold positions of power. The Powers expect those they dominate to submit to their authority as though the authorities are the anointed ones of God. Persons who stand in opposition to their authority may be accused of standing in opposition to God. This kind of self-serving religion is at the root of many of the most violent conflicts in the world today.

A theology of law and judgment also gives the leaders of institutional religion a key role in the politics of power and domination. A theology of law and judgment lends support to the methodology of violence. The "Just War Theory" (see the Glossary) is an example of the unholy alliance between institutional religion and the Powers. Chaplains in the military and Chaplains who preside over executions give the impression of legitimacy to acts of State-sponsored violence.

Although there are some who believe that politics and religion are to be kept separate, the truth is that they do not remain separate. Religion that supports the systems of domination is encouraged and even cultivated. Cooperation with the Powers is rewarded. Tax codes that provide huge tax breaks to religious institutions function as an effective deterrent to any serious challenge from the religious sector of society. When the cooperating religious institutions encourage participants to keep their focus on their own personal salvation they are not as likely to challenge oppression by the authorities in either the church or other structures of power. It should not be hard to see that in the long run, a theology of law and judgment requires submission, which in the minds of the Powers, is what God intended.

Like other self-interest groups, religious institutions engage in political lobbying related to matters which are perceived to be in their self-interest. For instance, the matter of using federal tax money for private religious education is a constant matter before the Congress and the courts. Religious groups may also promote political legislation that conforms with their doctrinal position such as the issues that abound around homosexuality, abortion and the pledge to the flag.

A Methodology of Violence

Both those who govern *and* those who are terrorists operate from the methodology of violence. They may try to convince others that they represent higher moral values, but both the Powers and terrorists utilize violence to achieve their goals. Both promote the erroneous idea that justice and peace is achieved through violence and that they are supported by divine authority in their pursuits. Walter Wink has properly called this the "myth of redemptive violence." It is deep within the psyche of our development as a nation and is, therefore, one of the most difficult matters to challenge in the mind of the oppressor.

Violence takes many forms. Poverty may be the most common manifestation of violence. Emotional deprivation or physical addictions are common forms of violence. Religious practices and doctrines are a source of violence when they are coupled with the demand to submit to authority or risk losing one's soul.

It is such an amazing paradox that while the Powers dominate through the use of violence they promote the belief that justice can be achieved through volunteerism or charity. While it sounds like a good thing to help those who are the less fortunate, the truth is that participation in charitable endeavors generally strengthens the systems of exploitation and domination. Charity is a subtle way to enlist support because it gives persons status in the domination system without changing any of the structures that are the source of oppression, persecution, or poverty. (see Chapter 5)

Jesus' intention was (and is) to change the very structures of society so that systemic evil, as well as individual sin, are both eliminated. Jesus would be saddened to see how we are content with substituting our limited acts of charity for taking up the struggle for justice.

Sharing God's kind of love with our neighbor is initiated by seeking justice and freedom for all. *Agape* is expressed through giving our heart and soul and mind and strength, i.e., our strongest expression of passion to the task.

Freedom and Justice will be achieved only when the oppressed are set free *and* the oppressors are also liberated. Our own liberation depends on our willingness to repent (turn around) from our cooperation with the oppressor.

We must escape from our entrapment in:

- The politics of power and domination
- A theology of law and judgment
- A methodology of violence

We must be converted to:

- The politics of liberation and freedom
- A theology of grace
- A methodology of non-violent agape

This is not the understanding of Jesus that I was taught in church and at the seminary. Belief in Jesus had to do with my personal salvation, not about political struggle. I was continuously cautioned not to mix politics and religion. By essentially keeping politics and religion separate I cooperated with the Powers and domination systems, including the church, the military and the authorities of government, etc.

My declaration that I was a Christian did not represent any threat to the domination systems at all.

Without a doubt the socio/political center of the world today is Washington, D.C.. If Jesus were alive today, he would weep over that city and once again say, "the things that make for peace are hidden from your eyes." Jesus would be weeping because we have not understood his invitation to "take up our cross" and engage in the politics of liberation and freedom.

Tragically, in the political climate in which we now live Jesus would be labeled as a terrorist for challenging the Powers. And even more tragic is that the authorities of the Church would be calling for Jesus to be crucified again.

In the next several chapters you will see how the *agape* of God revealed in Jesus reached out and touched my life. Jesus has won my heart and mind.

PART II
A New Christology

2

The Missing Chapter

Theology is how we express our understanding of God. The word "theology" is formed by the combination of two Greek words: *Theos* (God) and *Logos* (Word). Christian theology gets more complex as it includes what we say about: Christ (*Christology*); the Church (*Ecclesiology*); or the Holy Spirit (*Pneumatology*).

Christology explores the way in which Jesus came to be known as the Messiah or Christ. The joining of, "*Jesus*," and "*Christ*," to say, "*Jesus Christ*," is really a shortened version of expressing the belief that Jesus was the hoped-for Christ or Messiah written about in the Hebrew scripture.

It is important to keep in mind that they are not one and the same. "*Jesus*" is a historical figure. To say that Jesus is the "*Christ*", is an expression of faith.

My understanding of Jesus and my Christology went through many changes as I progressed from my childhood Sunday School classes, did post graduate work at a Methodist graduate school of theology, worked as a pastor for twelve years and then taught at Saint Paul School of Theology, a United Methodist seminary, for a period of fourteen years. Although the work at the seminary was very challenging and rewarding I felt called to a new vocation. It was on my fiftieth birthday in 1983 when I came to the firm belief that God was calling me to participate fully with those who live in poverty. In 1984 I gave up my credentials to the United Methodist Church as a pastor, resigned from my position as a professor at the seminary, and went to live in voluntary poverty with the poor in Nicaragua. For several years that small Central American nation had been suffering from a covert war waged by the Reagan Administration. U.S. citizens became more aware of the actions of the U.S. Government through what came to be known as the Iran-Contra Affair.

When Bishop Pedro Casaldàliga came to Nicaragua from Brazil in support of the struggle I was fortunate to be his driver and guide. On one occasion he said, "Once a person has been to the university or the seminary he can never be one of "*el pueblo*" again." By *el pueblo* (the people) he makes reference to the poor, the oppressed and the disenfranchised. I will use the term "*el pueblo*" to make that same reference throughout this book.

A major shift in my Christology emerged while living and participating with *el pueblo* in Nicaragua over a period of the next twelve years. Before going to Nicaragua I would have expressed my Christology in a very *orthodox* manner. In other words, my belief was basically in agreement with the Biblical theme of salvation, which is the prevailing approach to understanding Christianity in our society. Drawing upon that background I would have written my Christology in three chapters: *Incarnation, Crucifixion* and *Resurrection*:

1. **Incarnation**:

- Jesus was God with us in human form.

- Jesus was a charismatic itinerant teacher or Rabbi who preached love. and was able to do miracles.

- Jesus was a rebel who often got in trouble with the religious authorities for ignoring or breaking the laws of Jewish tradition.

- Jesus adopted the role of the "suffering servant" as portrayed by prophets in his Jewish Scripture; i.e., the Old Testament.

- Jesus was a religious Prophet and Mystic

2. **Crucifixion**:

- Jesus was condemned to death without a fair trial.

- Jesus was an innocent victim who was tortured and humiliated.

- Jesus accepted his death out of obedience to God.

- Jesus died on a Roman cross.

- Jesus was buried in a tomb.

- Jesus' sacrifice on the cross was a work of *Atonement* which brought about the reconciliation of sinful human beings with God. The how and the why of this reconciliation with God is expressed in several Theories of Atonement. *(see below)*

3. **Resurrection**:

- Jesus was raised by God from the dead and thereby achieved victory over sin and death.

- The resurrection of Jesus was confirmation that he was the Messiah.

- Jesus was taken to heaven and would intercede on our behalf with God.

- Jesus would return to establish the reign of God in this world.

- Easter, or the event of resurrection, was the cornerstone upon which the doctrine of the Christian Church was fashioned.

Atonement Theories

Atonement theories attempt to answer questions which are posed by the assumption that there is a basic alienation between human beings and God.

- What is required for alienated human beings to be reconciled with God or to the state of being be "*at one*" with God?

- If Jesus was such a wonderful miracle worker prophet and teacher, why did he have to die?

- Did Jesus have to die as a part of God's plan?

Three major theories about atonement are found in the history and tradition of the Christian Church. It is important to notice that they were each developed many centuries after the death of Jesus.

The *Ransom Theory* proposed by Origen in the Third century explained the atonement as a price or ransom paid by Jesus to God through the sacrifice of himself on the cross; or in some versions, the ransom paid by God to the Devil.

The *Anselmian Theory*, introduced by St. Anselm during the Eleventh century. The atonement was an act of satisfaction paid by Jesus to God who required perfect obedience to the law. Due to human sinfulness no person could fulfill this requirement except God's own son.

The *Abelardian Theory* promoted by Peter Abelard at the beginning of the Twelfth Century viewed Christ's death as such an ideal act of love that it is worthy of imitation and thus, by inspiring such a response of love in the sinner, may remove his sin.

No universal doctrine of atonement has ever been adopted. However, linking personal salvation to the atonement is what we have inherited through orthodox Christian tradition. Derivations following from the Ransom Theory continue to be the dominant approach to the atonement in most Christian churches today. Somehow the sacrifice of Jesus on the cross satisfies or pacifies God, so those who believe in Jesus will have the option of eternal life instead of eternal suffering or death. The faithful can look forward to their reward by going to Heaven instead of Hell.

Throughout my life I was never really at ease with *Salvation Theology*. This approach to theology did not seem consistent with the concept of the God revealed by Jesus, i.e., a God whose essential nature is defined by *agape*. Jesus believed that God's unconditional *agape* is available to each person in the here and now. I could not comprehend how this God would demand a sacrifice on the part of Jesus in order to reconcile the human community to God's self.

Where does the requirement that Jesus must suffer and die fit in? Even though it was part of the teaching and the tradition that shaped my life, I finally came to the conclusion that *it doesn't fit*! At the very least it places a "condition" on God's *agape*. Now I recognize that this kind of theology is part of the "mind of the oppressor" that I need to challenge.

The question remains, "Why did Jesus have to die?" A more coherent and convincing answer emerged for me as I learned more about the *Biblical theme of liberation* while living with *el pueblo* in Nicaragua.

For most of five centuries, *el pueblo* in Latin America have been indoctrinated with a theology based on the Biblical theme of salvation. They were taught to submit to both the authority of the Church and the State. If they wanted access to salvation they must accept Jesus as their personal Savior and receive the sacraments or "Means of Grace" exclusively through the Church. By accepting the injustices and oppression, which was their daily fare, they were promised the salvation of their souls and a better life in heaven after they died. While this tradition was primarily the tradition of the Roman Catholic Church it also fits for the most part with the doctrines of other institutional Christian Churches.

In Latin America it was the printing and distribution of the Christian Bible in the language of the people following World War II that opened a whole new understanding for *el pueblo* who were at the base of the socio-economic pyramid. Upon reading the story of Exodus they recognized that God was an active player in the political process in setting the slaves free from their captivity in Egypt. They could also see this same promise for their freedom in the political participation of God in and through the life of Jesus. This was a radical shift from hoping to go to heaven after one died. It took the fear away from an encounter with an angry judgmental God who may consign a person to a fiery hell if you didn't submit to the doctrines of the Church.

The recognition of the Biblical theme of liberation also meant that a faithful response to Jesus involves the believer in a process of constructing a new society which would bring forth life with dignity, justice and peace in the here and now. To do this would require total involvement in the political process. It was absolutely consistent with the perception that the primary message of Jesus was about pursuing the development of the Kingdom of God in this world with little emphasis on the hereafter.

Believing that God is a participant in the liberation process did not lead to the illusion that God would simply relieve them of their suffering in some miraculous way. Rather, with God on the side of the oppressed, *el pueblo* felt called to challenge the systems that cause oppression, injustice, suffering and death in the human community.

This understanding of God is radical, it is Biblical, and it is dangerous.

Any attempt to change the systems of injustice represents a threat to the Powers who govern this world. The recognition by *el pueblo* that God is engaged with us in the pursuit of justice is a source of strength and courage. The Biblical theme of liberation, does not offer the kind of security and comfort which is implied in the promises of Salvation Theology.

We have already noted that Jesus never saw any separation between religion and politics. Indeed, the true test of *integrity* is how a person unites these two facets of life. The teachings of Jesus, his acts of healing, the miracles ascribed to him and his confrontation with the authorities were always both political and religious. People saw this integrity in Jesus as he invited them to join him in the struggle for their own freedom.

I try to keep in mind that Jesus was not part of the Western Civilization and its Greek-Roman heritage which thrives on the scientific ordering of things. Western ideology is based on compartmentalizing or isolating distinct areas of life. For instance, it promotes the notion that religion and politics are discrete arenas of endeavor and are best understood by keeping them separate. Under this approach Jesus is de-politicized by being assigned almost solely to the arena of religion.

Salvation theology emerged from this Western ideology and works well within this frame of reference. Sin is essentially viewed as personal failure. Personal salvation and immortality become the focus of concern. The Church becomes the instrument through which God dispenses grace in this world. The Church promises to set one free from sin and death, but not from oppression and suffering.

Reflecting on the Biblical theme of liberation has led to some major changes in my Credo, especially with regard to my Christology. There is a wealth of scholarship identified as Liberation Theology which has emerged over the past fifty years and which I am not trying to summarize here. Although I value the research which comes from study and reading I am very clear that the opportunity to live and participate with *el pueblo* constitutes the more profound level of experience for me. Seeing the Biblical text through the eyes of *el pueblo* is one part of that transforming experience…but seeing it come alive as a living witness gives it genuine integrity.

The Atlantic side of Nicaragua is characterized by rugged mountains, jungles and great rivers that blend into coastal waterways and flow into the Caribbean Sea. The village of Paiwas is almost in the geographical center of Nicaragua. On Ash Wednesday, 1985, in this remote village of Paiwas, *el pueblo* were lined up to receive the "sign of the cross" on their foreheads. Most of them were campesino/as (peasants) who had fled from their farms and homes in the wake of the terrorist violence of the Contras who were financed, trained and controlled by the United States. These people already bore the "sign of the cross" in their hearts and souls. Their loved ones had been tortured, raped, kidnapped and murdered. I stood in line with them.

I had been in Nicaragua for seven months when I sent the following reflection back to my friends and family in the United States:

"I want to share a few thoughts about my faith journey. It would be better for me to share the confusion, the struggle, the anguish, the encounters with self and others, the joys, tears, laughter and lives that have brought forth these meager thoughts. I share them in the hope that you will add your own reflections to them as you progress through your faith journey.

"St. Francis of Assisi tells about the time when he became a knight. He says it was the only time he could remember when he pleased both his father and his mother at the same time. When he chose to live with poverty he said it took him two or three years to get all the armor off.

"Paulo Freire speaks of the way the oppressed take on the "mind of the oppressor." The oppressor controls the systems not only of commodities but of values. We are taught what is good, bad, beautiful, ugly, what is to be valued, what is worthwhile, what is important, etc. In short, the oppressor shapes the meaning of life for the oppressed. Freire calls for people to exercise Critical Consciousness which means to think for oneself, name and create one's own world based on one's own power and experience.

"The Old Testament tells of the liberation of the Hebrew people from slavery under the Pharaoh of Egypt. Apparently it took 40 years of wandering in the wilderness to get out from under the control of the "mind of the oppressor" or to get all of the "armor off" before they could enter the promised land.

"This reflects much of what I am experiencing right now. I am into a vast wilderness trying to shed the mind of the oppressor and trying to get all the armor off. To experience liberation always includes time in the wilderness with the accompanying temptations to believe that it was really better before, when living under the tyranny of Pharaoh. Pray for me in my wandering.

"I have come to a new understanding about the life of Jesus. It is simply this…Jesus was poor. He wasn't acquainted with poverty, exposed to poverty, concerned with poverty…he was poverty. This is what gave him his world view. If he was sinless it was because he never adopted the mind of the oppressor. He always spoke as one with authority, as one with a critical consciousness.

"Jesus was political. When you are poor you have no choice. He was always political because he had a constituency who followed his every action and word. So whenever he spoke or engaged in dialogue his message was primarily for the poor. The invitation to "take up your cross and follow me" is political. It was not directed to people as a general invitation to find a cross to take up…it was an invitation to those who already had a cross, the poor and oppressed.

"Jesus was fully human because he was poor. In my mind, I knew he was not rich, but I never really let him be poor either. In-so-far as that is true I dehumanized him. Because I made Jesus something other than poor and called that "human" (whatever that was), it also follows that I also never saw those who were poor as fully human. Those who were poor had to be something other than what they were; probably something better, more worthwhile. So I dehumanized the poor and I dehumanized Jesus and I dehumanized myself.

"Finally, one more image from Saint Francis. One tradition says that on his death bed, indeed with his last breath he spoke three words to his followers, "Poverty, peace, love." What did this mean? Was it some reflection on his vision of Christ? Was it the summary of his Credo? Is it a checklist for the faithful? Maybe it is all of these; or none of these. For me, these words have become a paradigm for my faith journey in the wilderness; my pillar of smoke by day and pillar of fire by night.

- **Poverty** is the position from which to gain the clearest perspective on life; the place where one can concentrate on the Powers with the most clarity.

- **Peace** is the goal toward which we are called to strive. There is no peace without justice. To seek peace is to give all against the aggression.

- **Love** is the means for achieving the reign of peace on earth. It is the source of power in the battle against evil. And the gift of grace is knowing that "we can love because we have been loved."

"And the war goes on. It is Easter and Jesus says, "Peace be with you!""

Managua, Nicaragua
Easter 1985

As you can see the revision of my Credo began early in my experience with *el pueblo*. I am so grateful that they invited me into their lives.

In further consideration of my Christology I discovered that in the prevailing tradition that I had been taught which is primarily focused on Salvation Theology, an entire chapter in Jesus' life had been omitted. *The Biblical theme of liberation was missing.* The fact that Jesus developed a non-violent insurrection movement was hidden from my eyes.

I have come to a better understanding of Jesus by including this major segment of his story in my Credo: *Incarnation,* **Insurrection**, *Crucifixion,* ***Re-Insurrection***.

1. Incarnation:

- Jesus was fully human and reveals the potential that resides in all human beings.

- The man, Jesus, uniquely reveals God's nature. In this way we can say that God is incarnate in Jesus.

- Jesus was a teacher, a prophet, a mystic *and* a political activist.

2. Insurrection: *the missing chapter in traditional Christology*

- *Jesus was an insurrectionist* who initiated a political movement to bring about the Kingdom of God.

- Jesus' goal was to liberate his people from the oppression of the Roman Empire and from corrupt political and religious leaders of his nation who were cooperating with the oppression of their own people.

- Jesus rejected the role of a Messiah who, through the use of violence, would be victorious over the Roman oppressors and restore Israel to the prominence it once enjoyed under King David and King Solomon.

- Jesus adopted the role of the Suffering Servant described by prophets in the Old Testament.

- Jesus put his faith in the power of non-violent *agape* as a method to approach the struggle for justice and freedom.

3. Crucifixion:

- *Jesus was crucified because he was an insurrectionist.* He had seen many of his countrymen who had been tortured and killed in seeking to achieve freedom through violent insurrection. By going to Jerusalem he knew he would be facing the possibility of his own death on a Cross.

- The Cross was used by the Roman Empire to kill political prisoners with the intention of striking terror in the people and to discourage further attempts at insurrection.

- Jesus was abandoned by all of his followers, who did not understand his approach to insurrection through non-violent *agape*. Peter in particular failed to align himself with Jesus and take up his cross.

- Judas was in agreement with promoting an insurrection but by going to the authorities he was trying to force Jesus into an armed insurrection.

- Jesus represented a genuine threat to both political and religious authorities.

- As an act of pacification Pilate gave the crowd a choice of naming one political prisoner to be released. By choosing Barrabas instead of Jesus the people placed their hope for liberation in violence.

- Pilate identified Jesus as the "King of the Jews." While revealing the true political nature of his encounter with Jesus it was also an act of mockery aimed at the Chief Priests who had called for Jesus crucifixion.

- Jesus died on the cross and was buried in a tomb.

4. Re-Insurrection:

- The insurrection movement Jesus initiated was thrown into confusion and disorder when he died on the cross. Immediately following the death of Jesus his disciples were in dispersion. Jesus' goal of gaining freedom through a non-violent insurrection seemed doomed.

- The miracle that took place is that the insurrection movement did not end with the death of Jesus. His followers came back together and reported stories of post-crucifixion encounters with a resurrected Jesus.

- Jesus had become the "Messiah" for the original group of followers because his presence and his message lived on in their hearts and minds.

- What occurred after the crucifixion and death of Jesus should be understood as *Re-Insurrection*, rather than *resurrection*. His followers were inspired to continue the struggle for justice based upon the example of non-violent insurrection that Jesus modeled for them.

- Jesus becomes our Christ or Messiah when we choose the cause of justice and freedom by following his model; i.e., the *Politics of Liberation and Freedom*.

Jesus was not only a martyr but a model. He had shown his followers the power of non-violent *agape* by going to the cross. Encounters with Jesus after his crucifixion all point to the continuation of the insurrection. While Jesus' followers had all failed to understand Jesus prior to his crucifixion they now came to experience the power of God's *agape* to conquer their fear of violence and death.

Jesus had not won the hearts of the Roman oppressors. Jesus also failed to win the hardened hearts of the religious and national authorities. However, Jesus had won the hearts and minds of a small band of followers who caught the vision that all things are possible with a God who participates fully in the struggle for liberation and freedom.

What brought these followers back together was not the hope of personal salvation. Before Jesus was crucified he had been both their political and spiritual guide in the struggle to free their homeland. What was inspiring them was the vision that the insurrection which Jesus initiated could be continued by them. Jesus did not come back from the dead and assume the physical leadership of the insurrection. In the absence of Jesus it was now up to them.

There cannot be any successful insurrection without inspiration, the indwelling of the Spirit. Jesus was inspired and held firm to the belief that God was with him all the way in the struggle for the liberation of his people. These early followers of Jesus remembered that he had promised that the Spirit would be with them to instruct and guide them. Jesus had assured them that they would actually do even greater things than he had done.

Jesus became the Christ for this little band of followers because he provided the example of how to struggle. Jesus had been the one who fulfilled the role of the hoped for Messiah by assuming the role of the Suffering Servant. Jesus revealed that the very nature of God is *agape*. Jesus revealed that this kind of love casts out fear. Jesus showed that *agape* overcomes the domination Powers of this world whose basic control over people comes through fear and the threat of death.

Through the various stories of post-crucifixion encounters with Jesus they came to believe that death is not the end of the relationship with God. They came together and concluded that God had validated Jesus' approach to the struggle by raising him from the dead. The narratives which tell of post-crucifixion experiences with Jesus became the cornerstone around which this small band of believers made the choice to follow his model and engage in the *re-insurrection*.

If his followers had abandoned the political struggle the memory of Jesus would have fallen away. If the movement had submitted to the model of violent insurrection Jesus would have been remembered as just one more martyr.

However, because this small band of believers placed their lives on the line by engaging in the re-insurrection, the stories of Jesus were recalled. They tried to remember his teaching even though they had not understood its deeper significance when he was still among them. The stories were shared. Some of the stories were written down. At that time they did not understand that they were writing "Scripture."

This little band of people had discovered the freedom which results from embracing non-violent *agape*. They never had any doubts about the dangerous nature of the undertaking they had accepted for themselves. Where they had been fearful they became fearless. The *re-insurrection* took the form of the "*Jesus Movement*." By its very nature it emerged as an underground or clandestine faction in the struggle to gain freedom for the homeland. The movement was having success in attracting others to the point that Jewish authorities wanted to stamp out the re-insurrection

If *atonement* was ever an issue it had been resolved even before Jesus was crucified. The Biblical theme of liberation reveals that God does *not require* some kind of payment or ransom before being willing to engage in the pain and suffering of the human community. The followers of Jesus were inspired by the vision of God as a full participant in their efforts to seek freedom and promote justice. As such, the Biblical theme of liberation maintains the integration of religion and politics.

It is in this part of the story that Saul of Tarsus enters the picture. Saul was a Jewish Pharisee who was intent on destroying the Jesus Movement. However, in the wake of a mystical religious conversion experience he proclaimed himself to be an apostle of "Christ." To mark this change in his life he also gave himself a new name, "Paul." I would remind the reader that while he was a Jew, he also brought with him the culture of the Hellenist world of Greece and Rome.

If Saul of Tarsus had remained the zealous persecutor of the re-insurrection he might have made it stronger. As the self-declared Apostle Paul, he succeeded in destroying the "*Jesus Movement*" from the inside by introducing Salvation Theology. In the next Chapter I will examine more in depth how Paul's influence dominated in the shaping of the Christian Church.

Identifying *insurrection* as the missing chapter in my Christology has brought about the—integration of religion and politics in my life. Changing the fourth chapter of my Christology from *resurrection* to *re-insurrection* was primarily due to my participation in the Christian Base Communities and in the development of the non-violent project, *La Insurrección Evangelica* The Gospel Insurrection), in Nicaragua.

"Base," as it is used here, refers to the people who live at the bottom of the socio/economic pyramid. While there may be some participants who are well off, the members are essentially made up of the *el pueblo*. These small groups, i.e., Christian Communities, gather to read and reflect on political and social reality in the light of the Gospel. Through "*praxis*," action-reflection, they determine what they must do to address injustice and bring about the reign of God on this earth. These groups are the source of Liberation Theology which promotes belief in a God who participates fully in the struggle for peace and justice.

Early in the armed insurrection by the Sandinistas to throw off the Dictator Somoza, the Christian Base Community movement in Nicaragua had adopted an understanding that, "There is no contradiction between Christianity and the Revolution." The goals espoused by both groups appeared to be parallel in their desire to create "a new man" and "a new society." They saw no contradiction because they had adopted the "just war theory." By accepting this approach to the struggle they had concluded that all other means had been tried and had failed. Therefore, taking up arms was necessary to achieve liberation. In this approach to achieving freedom, justice would come later in the process.

La Insurrección Evangelica (The Gospel Insurrection) is a project which was developed during the 1980's by the Christian Base Communities in Nicaragua. Following the lead of Father Miguel d'Escoto, who was at that time the Foreign Minister for Nicaragua, the leaders of the Christian Base Communities wanted to introduce the practice of non-violence in the struggle for their national independence.

Although the number of people who participate in these Christian Base Communities is a small percentage of the population, they represented a challenge to the authorities of the church as well as the Powers and domination systems. Their willingness to struggle for a new level of justice in the face of extreme hardship and suffering is nothing less than insurrection. With God at their side in the struggle they represented a genuine threat to the political and religious authorities in this world.

However, justice has not been realized in Nicaragua. Violence led to greater cycles of violence. The United States resumed control over this political uprising, which involved the integration of the Sandinista Revolution and the proponents of Liberation Theology. The people of Nicaragua are worse off than before. Poverty has slid further into misery. Once again the most powerful political and religious leaders of Nicaragua are cooperating as a client state with the United States which means more oppression of *el pueblo*. Worse and more to the point of this book is that the political and religious leaders who are embedded with the governing authorities in both Nicaragua and the United States continue to support the illusion that through the use of violence it is possible to realize peace and justice.

We need to recover the Jesus who challenged the Powers with non-violent *agape*. This understanding of how to express one's faith in God is Biblical; it is radical; it is dangerous, and it is political.

And yes, if we choose to follow Jesus, it means we are invited, as were the original followers of Jesus, to engage in the *Politics of Liberation and Freedom*.

3

The Politics of Liberation and Freedom

Jesus and his cousin, John, probably had long discussions about the oppressive situation in which they were living. They were both familiar with the checkered history of their national heritage in which their forefathers seemed to deviate from being faithful to God's original intentions for Israel, the *chosen people*.

They were both aware of how the prophets of old spoke truth to power when they saw corruption, hypocrisy and injustice on the part of their political and religious leaders. The prophets called for repentance and made it clear that the promotion of justice is the true expression of faithfulness in response to the God who brought them out of slavery in Egypt.

As part of *el pueblo*, Jesus and John were not only suffering from the harsh oppression of the Roman Empire but could see that corruption and immorality abounded in the leaders of their nation. What were they to do to fulfill their mission as a nation in the eyes of God? What did faithfulness require of them?

Through both preaching and offering the ritual of baptism John was calling for repentance from sin, i.e., to turn around and stop cooperating with the Powers of this world. Repentance meant to engage in doing God's will and to seek justice for both themselves and their oppressors. Those who were baptized by John were engaged in a renewal of both their religious and their political commitment. As serious as John was in calling for repentance he did not see himself assuming the role of the hoped-for Messiah. He did see this as the role that Jesus should endeavor to fulfill. They were both imbued with the image of the prophet Isaiah who pictured the Messiah as a "suffering servant."

Historically Jesus has been seen as blameless and without sin, so why would he participate in this ritual of cleansing and repentance and present himself to be baptized by John? One possible explanation is that Jesus submitted to John's baptism in order to identify himself totally with the struggle of *el pueblo*. Repentance is turning toward something, not just turning away from something. In the story of Jesus' baptism the metaphor of the descending dove represents the indwelling of the Spirit. This story suggests that Jesus was perceived as one who was inspired by the living Spirit of God.

After John baptized Jesus, the Spirit (not the devil) drove him into the wilderness where he was subjected to temptation. The temptations are those that are always offered by the Powers of this world and fall under the category of what we have been calling the mind of the oppressor. These are the temptations which are based on the *politics of power and domination.* Jesus' response to the temptations was the clear choice to stay faithful to God. In our Western world and the way religion has shaped our lives it is hard for us to understand that Jesus' responses to the temptations were political and not simply the exercise of religious conviction. Clearly, from this point in his life, Jesus' mission was predicated on the belief that God was actively present with him for guidance and for strength.

The Roman legions proclaimed "*good news*" as they returned triumphantly to Rome. Therefore, the use of this term in remembering the stories about Jesus had a loaded political connotation. Speaking of the *kingdom* and declaring *good news* would have been seen as a political action, indeed as a promise of victory for an oppressed people. When Jesus set out to promote the *Kingdom of God* he gathered together a small band to help him promote the *gospel…or the good news.*

The people probably wondered who Jesus was as he set about his mission. Accepting the fact that Jesus was fully human means that he had no distinct supra-human advantages. Indeed, by, simply acknowledging that he was more in tune with the Spirit does not make him less human. In a more positive sense, it reveals the possibilities that reside in our own human potential. Indeed, what Jesus was capable of doing we are also capable of doing. When Jesus was walking, teaching and healing he was *not* viewed or referred to as the *Son of God.* People did not run ahead of him saying, "Come see what the *Son of God* is doing in Galilee."

The premise that Jesus was the *Son of God* makes it more difficult to see him as being a truly human person This "religious" reading of his life was attributed to him well after he was crucified. This theological affirmation of Jesus as the *Son of God* picks up the theme of the "Christ of Faith," which was key to Paul's Christology and does not deal with the human nature of Jesus, which Paul basically ignored. Paul's version of Jesus as the Christ is the basis around which the Biblical theme of Salvation and the subsequent development of the Christian Church was developed.

The books which came to be included in the New Testament are developed in such a way that they reflected Pauline doctrine. For instance, people were invited to accept the belief that Jesus was the *Son of God.* John 3:16 is such a passage, *"For God so love the world that he gave his only son, so that everyone who believes in him may have eternal life."* Instead of seeing this as an affirmation of faith we are invited to see it as a fact. If we start with that assumption it influences everything else we read. Casting Jesus in the role of the Son of God has a tendency to keep us focused in the context of religion and obscures the socio/political reality of the story itself. It also tends to keep us focused on personal salvation rather than on the need for social, economic and political justice.

The selection of Jesus' core group was not done at random. No doubt Jesus had carefully considered persons to recruit for such an undertaking. He would have known who had been inclined to accept the perilous task of an insurrection which would seriously challenge the current power structure. Those who joined this endeavor looked to Jesus as both their spiritual leader and their political leader.

The core group of twelve disciples responded to Jesus' invitation with the hope that he was the one who could lead Israel back to freedom and political dominance. They had confidence that Jesus was such a leader. Jesus did not set out to create a church or a new religion. While Jesus was with them this group of disciples and other followers did not call themselves "Christians." Jesus was often disappointed that his followers did not understand his intention to challenge the domination systems of his world through a non-violent insurrection.

They did not respond to Jesus with the understanding that somehow he was going to save them from their sin by offering himself as a sacrifice on the cross. This kind of Christology based on the theme of salvation was introduced into the story after the crucifixion and as a result, much of what Jesus intended seems to have been lost. A number of questions arise as we try to follow the story:

- Why isn't the pursuit of justice through non-violent struggle a stronger theme in the record we read in the New Testament?

- What happened to the re-insurrection? Why did it disappear?

- How did the Jesus Movement become the Christ Movement?

- How did the Christ Movement become the Christian Church?

- How did the Christian Church become the Church of the Empire?

What appeared to be a failure to achieve his goals when Jesus died on the cross was not the end of the story. However, the essence of what Jesus had endeavored to accomplish took on new life. While small in numbers, the re-insurrection or Jesus Movement was having enough impact to be the object of persecution by the Jewish authorities.

Many people perceive the Day of Pentecost recorded in the Book of Acts as the beginning of the Christian Church. I do not agree. To grasp the true meaning of that day in relation to the Jesus Movement we must begin to see the "Pentecost" experience as political. The Day of Pentecost was a Jewish holy day and those who gathered on that occasion were all Jews. Many of them came to Jerusalem from other parts of the Mediterranean world for the occasion. For those faithful Jews who gathered that day, as for Jesus, politics and religion were totally integrated. Under the influence of the Spirit, Peter made the matter clear about why Jesus had been crucified. The Romans, with the collaboration of the Jewish authorities, crucified Jesus because he was a political activist challenging their authority.

Through the metaphor of the tongues of fire, the story reveals the expansion of the Jesus Movement beyond the small band of original believers. The experience of these Jewish people on the day of Pentecost was the verification that God, through the Holy Spirit, was a full participant in their struggle for freedom and liberation.

To say that people were "converted" on the day of Pentecost means they came to believe that the liberation of their Jewish homeland could be achieved in the manner which Jesus had taught, i.e., through non-violent insurrection. In that sense, Jesus becomes the hoped-for Messiah. This was not a conversion to save their souls; this was a conversion to engage in the re-insurrection. It was a conversion that followed in the same spirit of John's call for repentance. It meant turning around from cooperating with the Powers.

Those joining in the Jesus Movement or Re-Insurrection did not see themselves as starting either a new sect or a new church; and especially not a new religion. They were very clear, however, that they were engaged in a political struggle for their national independence and that the pursuit of justice was God's original purpose and mission for their nation.

Now that Peter had found his voice he became the chief spokesperson for the Jesus Movement. Even though Peter was thrown into prison he would not submit to the Jewish authorities who told him to stop doing what he was doing in the name of Jesus. Peter had decided to take up his cross. In this sense, Jesus was being resurrected. The non-violent insurrection Jesus initiated was going forth in his name. By being true to the power of *agape* Jesus had truly won his followers' hearts and minds.

The innovative life-style of this little band of believers represented their commitment to establish the Kingdom of God in this world. No one claimed private ownership of any possessions. Everything they owned was held in common and was distributed to each as any had need. These actions were intended to change social systems toward a more just society. They understood that these endeavors posed a genuine threat to both the political and religious authorities. This activity was not viewed by them as some temporary life-style while they awaited the "Second Coming" or return of Jesus who would then finish what he started. The concept of a Second Coming had not been introduced into the story at this early stage of the Jesus Movement.

Adopting the Politics of Liberation and Freedom was a dangerous undertaking, so they had to conceal some of their activities. Much of what they did took the form of an underground or clandestine movement. Because it was a relatively small movement made up of Jewish followers and because it was mostly viewed as a small sect engaged in an internal struggle within the Jewish community, it may not have attracted as much attention by the Roman authorities. The Romans had their attention focused on the activities of the Zealots who were still actively promoting a violent insurrection.

A major challenge to the Jesus Movement occurred when Saul of Tarsus entered the story. Saul was both a Roman citizen and a Jewish Pharisee. Saul believed that the Jesus Movement posed a serious threat to the tradition of Judaism. From Saul's perspective this subversive group was engaged in blasphemy and sacrilege. He was concerned that their political action may even have resulted in further intervention against the Jews by the Roman governor. He joined in the attempt to put an end to this movement.

Saul had the full support of the same Jewish authorities who had previously promoted the crucifixion of Jesus. The persecution of these followers of Jesus included throwing people in jail and even stoning some to death. It was violent enough that some of those involved in the Jesus Movement left Jerusalem to find safe haven in other parts of the country. In spite of the persecution the Jesus Movement was growing.

On one occasion Saul was traveling to the city of Damascus on a search-and-destroy mission to capture members of the Jesus Movement and haul them back to Jerusalem for punishment. While traveling on the road he had a mystical or "religious" experience which changed his life. He believed that he had experienced a personal encounter with the resurrected Jesus and that the ancient prophecy of a hoped-for Christ or Messiah had been fulfilled. To mark this change in his life he changed his name to "Paul." Although he changed his name it is important to remember that he still brought with him the culture of the Hellenist world of Greece and Rome.

It is important to remember that Paul never actually met the man Jesus. Paul had only his own private conversion experience from which he came to believe that this Jesus was "Christ." It is worth noting that:

- He never walked with Jesus.

- He never talked with Jesus or heard him speak of the Kingdom of God.

- He never struggled to understand Jesus' mission while Jesus lived.

- He was not a witness to the crucifixion of Jesus.

- He was not a part of the disappointment felt by Jesus' followers or the "dispersion" that followed the crucifixion.

- He was not one who experienced the post-crucifixion encounters with Jesus that called the original followers back together..

- He was not a part of the re-insurrection.

- He was not present at the experience of the Holy Spirit at Pentecost.

- He had not joined in the project of sharing life in a communal fashion.

Paul believed that his encounter was with the resurrected Jesus who had fulfilled the prophecy of the hoped-for messiah. He began to preach to the Hellenist Jews in the synagogues in Damascus saying that Jesus was "the son of God." His message was not well received and he escaped with his life. He went to Jerusalem and attempted to join the disciples who also did not trust him because of his reputation as the persecutor of the Jesus Movement. He then returned to his home town of Tarsus, which was located in what is now Turkey.

Based entirely on his personal mystical experience Paul identified Jesus as his personal Lord and Savior, the Son of God. This is the starting point of his conversion and the ending point as well. Somehow, for Paul, what Jesus had done on the Cross led to an atonement or reconciliation between God and sinful humankind. It is no wonder that it is through Paul that we learn of the idea that the renewal of a relationship with God is through faith by grace.

What was important for Paul was that he had found a new approach to religion. Belief in Jesus as the Christ became a matter of being saved from sin and death instead of a political model for engaging in the struggle against injustice and oppression. However, Paul was a Roman citizen so his "mind" was shaped not only as a Jewish Pharisee, but in large degree by the Hellenist culture in which he had lived. His conversion on the road to Damascus did not conflict with his cultural upbringing in the Hellenist culture (mind of the oppressor), which he never discarded and from which he never repented.

These are serious comments about a man whom the "Church Fathers" saw as the first missionary of the Christian Church. So, it is worth a brief analysis of the "mind of the oppressor" as it may be expressed through the Political Model of the Powers and see how it fits for Paul.

The Politics of Power and Domination:

- He was a Roman Citizen and depended on Roman laws to rescue him from conflicts he created through the promotion of his new religion.

- He believed in a God who, in the final analysis, would conquer through the use of power.

- He competed with other religions in promoting what he considered to be the right doctrine. Even if it is viewed as competition for the souls of believers it is still about having the right belief or being lost. Ultimately, this carried with it the goal of domination.

- He called on his followers to submit to the political authorities, who he believed had been placed in those powerful positions by God.

A Theology of law and judgment:

- Even with Paul's stress on being saved from personal sin by "faith through grace," the law remains the backdrop for his understanding of grace. As part of his development of his view of salvation he believed that a sacrifice was required to achieve a reconciled relationship with God. So Jesus became the Christ by satisfying God's requirements or ransom, i.e., another kind of satisfaction or legalism.

- He believed that there is no grace except through belief in Jesus as the Christ, which results in a theology of exclusion. Grace is, therefore, based on *proper belief,* which is just another form of legalism.

- The "means of grace," baptism and communion were under the control of the Church.

- He placed himself in opposition to the legalism of the Jewish tradition only to create another kind of discipline of correct behavior and morality.

A Methodology of Violence;

- The Kingdom of God would be achieved through violence with the unsaved consigned to a life of pain and death.

Paul became a man with a mission, especially to the gentiles or non-Jews. The development of Christian Churches became the structure through which to spread the new religion. However, this was intended as a temporary endeavor, because Paul believed that Christ, the Son of God, would return soon to finish what he had begun and usher in the reign of God. This belief in the "Second Coming" took away the imperative for any serious struggle for liberation. For many Christians it still does.

Caesar had a problem with this emerging Christian Church because the Christians would not acknowledge Caesar as God. This refusal had its political consequences. Actually the "Christians" made an easy target for Caesar's violence. The Christians only represented a small movement in terms of numbers with no ethic or national background to stand in the way of their persecution. Caesar's actions underscored what would happen to the Jews if they undertook a challenge to his Empire but the Zealots didn't get the message even then. For Paul and his followers it became more important than ever to hold onto the belief that Jesus would return soon and usher in the Kingdom of Heaven. The goal of the believers in Christ was to live with the kind of faithfulness and morality that would meet the requirements for salvation and eternal life.

Due to the placement of Paul's writings in the New Testament it is not clear to most readers that Paul's writings were being circulated well in advance of other writings recorded in the New Testament. In spite of the fact that Paul seems to have entered the story as a late-comer, the meaning of the resurrection as the key event in bringing about salvation was mostly shaped by his preaching and writing. Therefore, as we have previously noted, later writers of the New Testament wrote their accounts already shaped by Paul's version of Christ.

Due primarily to the influence of Paul, it was only a matter of a few years, perhaps a decade, before the post-crucifixion attempt by the Jesus Movement to achieve a non-violent insurrection lost its focus. Peace would be something to experience in heaven rather than on this planet. Or, possibly, it would be an experience of the faithful at the time of Jesus' Second Coming. Even more regretably, *the name of Jesus ultimately came to be identified with the promotion of violence rather than liberation, oppression rather than justice, and with domination rather than peace.*

One of my colleagues says I am too hard on Paul. While he also disagrees with Paul on many matters, he says, "You have gone too far if you push me to the point where I have to defend Paul." I reminded my friend that although I find many issues with Paul, I respect him as a man who genuinely lived his Credo and felt that he had received a special calling to be an apostle.

Paul had such a profound influence on the early shaping of the Christian Church that his letters or epistles were included in the Canon of the New Testament and given the status of Sacred Scripture. However, when Paul was writing his letters to the new believers in the "Christ of faith," he *did not* perceive of himself as writing sacred scripture. He would be amazed to find, that based on a literal reading of the Bible, there are Christians who attribute the same significance to his writing as they attribute to the sayings of Jesus.

I was brought up on Salvation Theology. Paul's concept of being saved by grace through faith was at the heart of what I was taught. After all, he was the scriptural hero of the Protestant Reformation. I was taught that Christianity was all about religion; being saved by grace through faith, being baptized in the name of the Father, the Son and the Holy Spirit, and joining the Church whose mission was focused on converting others so they could also be saved, with a little charity thrown in on the side for good measure.

I believe that God can speak to us through the narratives, events, poetry and prayers recorded in the Bible. The writers whose contributions were incorporated into the Bible were basically sharing their Credo at the times they were writing. At times they were also attempting to add to or correct what others had already written. Paul did this as part of his Credo; he reinterpreted his sacred scripture, the Torah and the Prophets (Old Testament), to make his case that Jesus was the Son of God and the hoped-for Christ.

The most detailed expression of Paul's Credo may be found in the letter he wrote to the Christians in Rome. Bible scholars date this letter around AD56, which was at least twenty years after the date when Jesus was crucified. Paul begins by giving his credentials and stating a brief summary of his Credo:

> "Paul, a slave to Jesus Christ and called to be an apostle, set apart for the gospel of God, which he promised beforehand through his prophets in the holy scriptures, (Old Testament) the gospel concerning his Son, who was descended from David according to the flesh and declared to be Son of God with power according to the Spirit of holiness by resurrection from the dead, Jesus Christ our Lord, through whom we have received grace and apostleship to bring about the obedience of faith among all the Gentiles for the sake of his name..." (Romans 1:16)

While Paul makes the argument that a person is saved by faith through grace, he also makes salvation exclusive by saying that *only* those who have faith in Jesus Christ will have access to God. This concept is directly tied to Paul and his concern with personal salvation. I am convinced that Jesus never claimed to be the Son of God. Where Jesus was concerned with the Kingdom of God, Paul was concerned with the Kingdom of Heaven.

Paul had some wonderful things to say about how to remain faithful once you find Christ in your life. Things like, "Let love be genuine; hate what is evil, hold fast to what is good; love one another with mutual affection; outdo one another in showing honor..."Contribute to the needs of the saints; extend hospitality to strangers..."Do not be overcome by evil, but overcome evil with good." (Romans 12)

And Paul also had some things to say which I believe are antithetical to the teaching and mission of Jesus. Following the encouragements listed above he admonishes the believers in Rome to, "Let every person be subject to the governing authorities; for there is no authority except from God, and those authorities that exist have been instituted by God. Therefore whoever resists authority resists God..."For the same reason you also pay taxes, for the authorities are God's servants, busy with this very thing." (Romans 13)

A bit later in this letter he reminds them that the Second Coming is getting closer and is the reason for keeping the faith. He tells the Christians in Rome, "Besides this, you know what time it is, how it is now the moment for you to wake from sleep. For salvation is nearer to us now than when we became believers; the night is far gone, the day is near." (Romans 13)

It is fun to imagine how Paul would re-write his Credo if he was in our world today. Given what has occurred in the history of Christendom he would grieve at the fractured nature of what he had identified as the Body of Christ. He would recognize that the anticipated "End Times" or the Second Coming of Jesus has not occurred and would revise his own Credo accordingly.

My hunch is that Paul would still put a great deal of emphasis on personal salvation, but I wonder if he would still have an exclusive view of gaining access to God only through faith in Christ. As a man of integrity he would be dismayed with how his vision of Christ has been used to give scriptural support to the Church as one of the domination systems as well as being used as a source to legitimate the Church's cooperation with and participation in the Politics of Power and Domination.

I believe Paul would follow his own admonition to, "Let love be genuine, abhorring evil, cleaving to the good." Indeed, I believe that Paul would join the re-insurrection carried forth by the Jesus Movement and become a force in promoting the Politics of Liberation and Freedom.

Along with the Paul's influence on the shaping of the stories of Jesus as the Christ another historical event happened that had great influence on how these early Christians wrote their Gospel accounts. As we have seen, around AD66 the Zealots engaged in a violent uprising against the Roman occupation of Israel. The Roman emperor, Nero, sent troops to put down the uprising. By AD70 the Temple had been destroyed and Jerusalem had been devastated.

The Gospel of Mark was written during this period of violence and conflict. The Gospels of Matthew and Luke were written shortly after the destruction of Jerusalem. The Gospel of John was written after the turn of the Second Century, some seventy years after the crucifixion of Jesus. Following the lead of Paul it seems that each Gospel writer focused on religion as a way to promote Jesus as the Christ. Jesus was recalled as a Savior who could save people from sin with the hope of life after death.

The doctrine that viewed the Resurrection of Jesus as proof that his sacrifice had reconciled humankind to God became the central focus as the Christian Church developed. As such, a theology centered on salvation displaced the historical acts of Jesus whose mission was based on the struggle for liberation. Due to this shift, the life and death of Jesus becomes a dramatic story of a religious martyr rather than that of a passion-filled political liberator.

I am convinced that if it had not been for the re-insurrection we may never have heard the name of Jesus. Those original believers who formed the early Jesus Movement obviously had various mystical experiences of post-crucifixion encounters with Jesus. These stories became the resurrection narratives, which in themselves would not have kept the story alive. What kept the story alive was the choice to continue in the footsteps of Jesus and engage in the ongoing insurrection.

Jesus showed them how to speak truth to power. He showed them how to share *agape,* even with the enemy. He showed them the power of non-violence. He showed them the depth of his passion. The original group of followers were moved by the depth of his faith in God. They were inspired by his willingness to trust his belief in the power of non-violent *agape* by going all the way to the cross.

The miracle is not that God raised Jesus from the dead, not at all. The true miracle is that that these humble followers got the message and became aware of their own capacity for drawing on *agape* as the source of their own passion for liberation.

There can be no insurrection without inspiration and they were inspired. Jesus knew that passion without spiritual grounding is not enough. It can easily lead to distortion. He invited them to wait for the Spirit to guide them as it had guided him. It was essential that these followers have their own first-hand experience of Spiritual inspiration. *Pentecost* was the time when the Jesus Movement surfaced under the guidance of the Spirit.

They began to recall and record what Jesus had said and done. However, the telling of the story had to be told in the light of the destruction of Jerusalem and the Temple. Now they had to share their stories in a manner that would not instantly result in a violent response on the part of the Roman Empire.

So, as I read the story, the Jesus Movement loses its heart as the Biblical theme of liberation. The Pauline vision of the Kingdom of Heaven gives way to the emergence of a salvation-oriented Christian religion which is submissive to the domination system. As the Christian Church under the form of a new Religion spread, it set in motion controversies that were debated in the search for a standard set of doctrines. These controversies primarily centered on the issue of whether Jesus was divine or human. The question being debated was how to explain that Jesus was the Son of God, even though Jesus never made that claim for himself.

The Canon of the New Testament, or what has come to be seen as Sacred Scripture, was finally determined by the Bishops of the Christian Church who had made their peace with Caesar. The agreement for what would be included in or excluded from the New Testament wasn't settled until around the year AD367. The bishops also found a way to confirm the "Church" as sacred in the process. They would have us believe that it was the Church that was born at Pentecost. They would insert the story of Jesus confirming Peter in his role as the "rock" on which the church would be built.

As a result of the so-called conversion of the Roman Emperor, Constantine, in the 4th Century A.D. the Christian Religion became the official religion of the empire. There are mixed reports about the conversion of Constantine. One version is that he had a vision or a dream which instructed him to use the symbol of the cross on the battle standards of his army going into battle. In the vision he was promised that by leading it the cross he would achieve victory in the ensuing battle. He was successful in battle and attributed the victory to the power of the God of the Christians. Although Constantine did not have a deep understanding of the Christian faith he did understand how to use this new religion to his political advantage.

The Christian Church became an instrument of imperial policy. There is evidence that Constantine even entrusted some government functions to Christian clergy. Constantine saw how important it was to maintain peace in the empire by bringing some resolution to controversies being debated by the various Bishops of the Christian Church. It was Constantine who called for the First Ecumenical Council of the Christian Church in the year 325. He made it clear that the leaders of the church needed to "work it out and get along." So it was from this council that the first version of the Nicene Creed was formulated affirming the doctrine that Jesus had always been part of the Godhead. In other words, Jesus had always existed as the Son of God in the Trinity, again, something that Jesus never claimed. Other opinions were submerged to achieve political stability.

Athanasius, who was later the Bishop of Alexandria, played a major role in this council. The Canon of the New Testament was based on a list developed by Athanasius. This did not occur until after the Christian Religion had become the official Religion of the Empire, which is the role it continues to play in today's world of politics and religion.

While one might argue that the Christian Church had finally overcome the Roman Empire, I would argue the opposite to be true. The Empire prevailed over the Christian Church which had its original origins in the Jesus Movement. Let me briefly summarize this history:

- The Jesus Movement lost its way when it became the Christ Movement.

- The Christ Movement lost its way when it identified itself as a "church" and not as a liberation movement.

- The Church lost its way when it identified its mission to promote Christianity as a religion.

- Christianity lost its way when it became a major player in the *Politics of Power and Domination;* preached a *Theology of Law and Judgment;* and cooperated with *a Methodology of Violence*

Even still we must feel grateful that the story was not lost. For those who have eyes to see and ears to hear Jesus still reaches out to us from the New Testament. Our task is to learn how to read the sacred story and clearly see the political significance of Jesus' life. When we do, we will better understand Jesus' admonition to, *"Enter through the narrow gate. For the gate is narrow and the road is hard that leads to life, and there are few who find it."*

Some traditions of the Christian Church draw on the Paul's image that the Church is the "Resurrection Body of Christ." What a difference it would make, if instead we could conceive of the community of believers as the *Re-Insurrection Body of Jesus.*

To engage in the re-insurrection we must discover our own passion for justice, and commit to bringing non-violent love to the struggle for freedom and liberation.

Indeed, we must be willing to take up our cross and follow Jesus.

4

The Trinity

The doctrine of the Trinity is not really addressed in any specific way in the Bible. Still, for those who want to have an amusing theological exercise, just go to the internet and type in the word Trinity and you will get more Biblical references than you can walk your way through in a month of Sundays.

In Christian tradition, the concept of the Trinity is in reference to the belief that God has revealed God's self to us in three ways: as the Father, Son and Holy Spirit. The challenge in the attempt to develop creedal statements ran into the complexity of trying to maintain monotheism and yet express three different ways of encountering God in the context of Christian mythology.

My Credo may make more sense to you if I share how I have come to view the concept of the Trinity expressed as: God the creator, Jesus the liberator, and God the Spirit, present with us for guidance and for strength.

When we speak of God

To speak of God at all is to speak of a mystery around which we cannot actually wrap our finite minds. We are finite beings and cannot even encompass the concept or the being or person we allude to as God. In attempting to define God we inevitably address a concept that goes beyond our human abilities to comprehend.

If we speak of God as though we can define the term in anything more than symbolic language then we become the creators of God. Historically the postulation of God has been accompanied with vain attempts to resolve the mystery by speaking of God in terms which are abstract in the extreme, i.e., all-powerful, infinite, all-knowing, omnipotent, omniscient, higher power, creator, nature, etc.

The idea that we can enter into a relationship with God will always require a leap of faith. It will inevitably be a mystical experience that will not pass the test of scientific proof. So, the task of speaking of God, our theology, must be approached with a deep sense of humility.

When we speak of Jesus

We can readily speak of the human person known to us as Jesus. The abstract becomes real to us and understandable within our own human capacity for knowing. Even our human ability to create images can be useful. As humans we are capable of pursuing truth through analogy and metaphor as well as through scientific experimentation.

When we say that God is revealed through Jesus, we are really saying that some distinct perceptions about "what God may be like" can be formed by our observations of Jesus. It is in that sense that we say God was incarnate in Jesus. This is quite a different thing from saying that Jesus is God. The claim that Jesus was the Son of God is even an expression of faith which distorts our observations of his humanity. To say that Jesus was divine may imply that he was not truly and fully human like us. This characterization of Jesus attributes supra-human capabilities to him that are not available to an ordinary person's limited human abilities. We must also caution ourselves not to engage in simply projecting totally human characteristics on God.

Like us, Jesus lived in an historical context. During the time Jesus lived the perception of the world was related to a three-story universe: heaven above, earth in the middle, and hell or darkness below. These conceptual images no longer define the nature of the universe for us. However, there has been little change in the issues confronted in the human experience. Systems of domination, injustice, oppression and the desire in the human heart for justice and peace are still with us. The struggle continues.

We must come to see a genuine potential for our own human development in the capacity for passion and spirituality manifested by Jesus. What Jesus did illustrates that we are also capable of doing through the inspiration of the Holy Spirit.

When we speak of the Holy Spirit

To speak of the Holy Spirit involves us in another experience of mystery beyond the finite power of human intelligence. We are dealing with a concept that we as human beings cannot easily fathom. Here again we must approach what we consider to be sacred with great humility.

Human beings often attest to having spiritual experiences that may be expressed as having a relationship with forces that are supra-human. These mystical experiences point to a power beyond the human self, which is *invisible but discernible*. The connection is sufficiently real so that as humans we may speak of the leading of the Spirit in our attempts to understand the nature and will of God.

Jesus was such a mystic and encouraged people to open themselves to the guidance of the Holy Spirit, primarily through prayer.

The word "inspiration" refers to the indwelling of the Holy Spirit both in our personal and our social lives. I believe it is the function of the Spirit to help us see Jesus with clarity. By keeping our focus on Jesus I believe the Spirit helps us to understand not only the nature of God but also the nature of humanity.

At times the Holy Spirit invites us to a "knowing" of something which goes beyond our capacity to explain in simple human terms. At other times it seems that the Holy Spirit invites us to simply participate in the mystery of the creation process itself. Mostly the Holy Spirit invites us to see, feel, and know things with which we can identify as part of our human condition of finitude.

The concept of the Trinity aids us in recognizing the love of God, *agape,* as it continues to be made flesh in our contemporary lives. It takes all three images to encompass the mystery: God the creator, Jesus the liberator, and the Spirit present with us for guidance and for strength. In all three ways we have the revelation of a God who is an active participant in the liberation process.

As was the case for the early followers of Jesus, to succeed in creating the Kingdom of God on earth depends on being thus inspired.

5

Love of Neighbor

The following is an exchange reported between a scholar and Jesus:

> The scholar asks, "Of all the commandments, which is the most important?"
> Jesus answers, "First; you shall love the Lord your God with all your heart and
> with all your soul and with all your might. The second is this; you shall love
> your neighbor as yourself."

Jesus knew his Torah. He had been well schooled in what was sacred scripture
for the Jewish people. In a culture that was overrun with legalisms and com-
mandments, Jesus kept it simple.

In the early 1980's, when Dr. Roy Sano was a professor at Pacific School or
Religion, we both were teaching at Hawaii Loa College on Oahu. Sometimes we
combined our classes and during that summer Dr. Sano gave a lecture that had a
strong influence on my spiritual journey. I recorded it in my notes as: *The Poverty
Line vs. The Power Line.* I have put my own "spin" on what he shared so I apolo-
gize for any misrepresentation or distortion I may introduce in describing what
he said in his lecture. The discussion that follows should be attributed to me and
not to him. A few years later Roy Sano was elected to be a Bishop of the United
Methodist Church.

Most of the values we embrace are not taught in the classroom but are shaped
informally in the process of our socialization. One of the things we learn early is
that we can easily evaluate how we are doing in the socio/economic structures by
assessing where we are in relation to the *"Poverty Line."* If we are doing better
than those we see at the poverty line we can feel okay about ourselves.

To determine what constitutes the "poverty line" is no easy task. The attempt
to define the poverty line on the part of the Census Bureau and the U.S. Government Department of Health and Human Services, along with other social agencies, results in a very complex set of measurements and guidelines. As such, the
poverty line is not all that well defined for most of us.

Based on simple observations it is enough for many persons to determine that there are those who are "less fortunate" than themselves. Often one hears people say that they should not complain because there are others who are, "worse off" than they are themselves. This kind of observation may originate from a need to believe that he or she is "better off," or it may come from a sense of compassion. In either case it is a way of placing oneself in the socio/economic pyramid.

In our society stigma may be attached to a person identified as being at the poverty line or below. Individuals may also agree with cultural norms that suggest that living in poverty is a matter of personal failure. Self-judgment can be even harsher than that of our peers if we see ourselves as sliding into poverty rather than climbing up the ladder of success.

Paulo Freire would identify this informal shaping of our values as the formation of the "mind of the oppressor." For instance, reference to the "American Dream" promotes the illusion that one can succeed at whatever they want to do simply through desire and hard work. This dream may be more of a nightmare for the majority of the population, especially for those who are born at the bottom rung of the socio/economic structures. A further misconception which adds to the burden of being poor is the widely held notion that individuals can and must get out of poverty through their own personal effort.

By placing ourselves higher in the socio/economic pyramid we also make judgments about our own status in the society. Sadly, we might even arrive at the conclusion that we are not only "better off," but that we are in fact, "better than" others. This is the nature of "Classism" and it is rampant in our society.

The informal teaching of the culture which helps us conform to the mind of the oppressor also promotes ethical principles about appropriate ways to relate to those who live in poverty. Basically we are taught that we are supposed to *help* those who are less fortunate than ourselves. This *help* usually expresses itself through charity, benevolence and volunteering.

We also learn that we can engage in doing charitable acts without placing our own social well-being at risk. We may even be encouraged to see how our participation in charitable endeavors may enhance our own social status. The decision to get involved with helping the poor is frequently undertaken with a great deal of caution. Many individuals, as well as institutions, want to be sure that they are not being "conned" or "ripped off" by those they have set out to help.

Rather than genuine compassion or the expression of genuine concern for others, our actions may be motivated by indulging our own ego needs. Needless to say, self-gratification is not the best way to express our concern for others, especially *el pueblo*, the poor and disenfranchised. Meeting our own needs in the process of giving help results in another form of exploitation. A careful examination of our own motives for engaging in acts of charity may help to reduce the possibility of abuse to ourselves or others in the process.

Charity, benevolence and volunteering are ethical principles actively promoted by churches, professional organizations, corporations and governmental agencies. In other words, our understanding of how we relate to those who are the less fortunate is constantly being shaped by the Powers. Adopting these norms is generally done without any serious reflection on the fact that we are cooperating with the mind of the oppressor. Insofar as we adopt these values as a way to help the poor we are either being deceived or deceiving ourselves.

When two of my seminary colleagues and I organized a course based on Paulo Freire's book, *The Pedagogy of the Oppressed,* I was introduced to the importance of three little words: *"to," "for"* and *"with."* Freire made the point that when one engages in doing something *"to"* others it is generally based on having *power over* those persons. Doing something *"for"* another person would seem to suggest some level of compassion or charity. However, Freire believes it is a more subtle way of exercising *power over* that person. At the very least it still represents a power differential in the relationship.

Freire develops the concept of sharing power *"with"* others. In this approach one respects the capacity of others to take action in their own behalf. This approach is an attempt to avoid subtle or hidden forms of domination. This is no easy task when working with a culture like ours that promotes success or failure based on competition and power over others. In the final analysis we should be motivated by love and the desire to participate with others in their striving for life with dignity.

Rather than looking at the *Poverty Line* as a way to express our compassion or concern for the poor, Bishop Sano calls on us to look at the *Power Line.* As Christians he says we are invited to do battle with the Powers and domination systems of this world. He says that Christ is the Lord of History, not the Lord of the Manor (the church). In other words, Bishop Sano wants us to see that the work undertaken by Jesus was political and not simply religious.

By changing our focus to observe the domination systems of exploitation and oppression we will see that they are responsible for most of our poverty, and in many cases depend on poverty for the maintenance of economic wealth and privilege. Charity masks the problem and helps to maintain the status quo without addressing the root causes of the poverty. Because charity does not challenge or change the structures of society, the attempt to express compassion for the poor through charity actually results in giving aid to the rich and powerful. Let me say that again: The attempt to express compassion for the poor through charity actually results in giving aid to the rich and powerful. It changes nothing and drains off energy and resources which may be better utilized to fight the causes of poverty and oppression.

Perhaps a greater wrong which is perpetrated through charity and welfare programs is the violence we are doing to *el pueblo* by robbing them of their sense of dignity and self-worth. A man in the poverty neighborhood where I lived in Kansas City expressed his resentment about the distribution of food baskets or free meals at Thanksgiving and Christmas. He viewed these actions as simply being reminders of how poor he was and did nothing to change his situation. He could see that charity is an integral part of the oppressive systems that victimize people, and not the solution.

Jesus was not offering charity. The passion we see revealed in Jesus was his unwavering participation with his neighbors in the struggle for freedom and justice. Standing with the "least of these" he spoke truth to power. Through his teaching, healing and miracles he was disclosing the failure of the domination systems of his day. The Kingdom of God will only come as we dismantle the systems of oppression and injustice and create a new order where justice prevails. This is what Jesus set out to do through political and social insurrection. Ultimately, for Jesus, it meant taking up the cross.

No matter where we find ourselves in the socio/economic pyramid we can turn from cooperating with injustice by changing our focus from the *Poverty Line* to the *Power Line*. Where we are standing makes a huge difference in what we see when we observe the *Power Line*. We may discover that we benefit from the way the systems are structured and not just from our own hard work or good fortune. We may recognize that changes are necessary to bring about justice and reduce suffering in the world and at the same time resist giving up our own privileges in order to accomplish these changes. We may also recognize that if we challenge the systems of privilege we may lose the status we currently enjoy.

I do not want to romanticize the life of *el pueblo*. People who live in poverty are as capable of adopting the mind of the oppressor as other members of society. However, an amazing level of wisdom also comes from those who experience the injustice of poverty that accompanies their day-to-day lives. If we are not open to learning from them about their experience of reality, we will continue to look to ourselves and/or the Powers for direction. We know how the domination systems can distort the truth. We know that they are capable of calling that which is "evil...good," and worse, calling that which is "good...evil."

Since I have been participating with *el pueblo* at the *Poverty Line* it has been my experience that:

- I can see the *Power Line* a lot more clearly.
- I can read the scripture with more comprehension.
- I understand Jesus better.
- I relate to my neighbor with more honesty.
- I am more willing to acknowledge my own spiritual poverty.

Jesus invited the people to join him in making the changes that would lead to a new society called the Kingdom of God. His passion for justice was not expressed through acts of charity. The passion of Jesus was expressed through non-violent, non-cooperation with the Powers. Jesus demonstrates that *agape* has the power to cast out fear. When fear is gone the oppressor has no further control over *el pueblo*.

The story of Bishop Oscar Romero of El Salvador is an amazing story of a man who became fearless in the face of the threat of violence and death in his own search for justice and truth. It is a compelling story of how learning to love one's neighbor changes everything. It is a powerful illustration of what can happen when the Politics of Liberation and Freedom is taken seriously.

Oscar Romero was born in El Salvador in August 1917 and by the time he was thirteen years old he was already committed to the vocation of the priesthood. He was ordained in 1942 and was known for his acts of charity and compassion. In 1974 he became the Bishop of Santiago de Maria. He held conservative views and was not in agreement with the position taken by the 1968 Conference of Roman Catholic bishops at Medellin, Columbia, where they determined that in "the struggle between the rich and the poor, the Church must make a preferential option for the poor."

Many of his priests had adopted this liberation approach in their ministry. Bishop Romero felt that the actions taken by his priests were responsible for much of the violence that was occurring in the struggle with the government of El Salvador. He asked his priests and *el pueblo* to be less aggressive in their confrontation with the authorities. He appealed to them to be patient because he believed that through the expression of Christian compassion and charity all of these matters could be resolved.

Three years later, in 1977, Romero was named the Archbishop of San Salvador. The twelve families who dominated the political and economic policies of El

Salvador had no problem with the appointment of Bishop Romero. Politically, it was a safe choice. Within a few weeks of his confirmation as Archbishop one of his priests, Rutilio Grande, was murdered in cold blood, along with a boy and an old man.

Bishop Romero attempted to seek help from the system with which he had always cooperated. He took his appeal to the President of El Salvador and other leaders of the government. He was still looking at this event through the mind of the oppressor as he sought answers from those in positions of power. In response to his appeals he got promises, but no results. He pushed, pleaded, was patient, waited, and prayed, but he got no results.

Bishop Romero's focus had shifted from the *poverty line* to the *power line*. Bishop Romero's true conversion occurred when he called for justice in the case of Rutilio Grande's murder. He did not find the response of justice he had hoped for and which he assumed would be forthcoming just for the asking. He was calling for justice and not backing off when he got no results. It was then that he discovered the true nature of systemic evil. The Powers turned their anger and violence on him.

The more Bishop Romero called for justice, the more violence was aimed at him and his people. More priests were murdered. The scales fell from his eyes and he began to see the reality in which he lived without filtering it through the mind of the oppressor. He began to participate with *el pueblo* in the struggle. His strategies were consistent with Jesus' methodology by engaging in non-violent direct action. He became the voice of the poor. He documented the atrocities and reported them during his regular Sunday homilies, which were broadcast throughout the country on the radio.

In 1979, using well-documented dossiers of the atrocities against *el pueblo*, Bishop Romero presented his findings to the Vatican and the Pope in Rome. His appeal was ignored. Bishop Romero was being isolated by other Bishops and powerful interests in the Church. The media and press joined in attacking him for his stand with the poor and oppressed. Romero even wrote a letter to Jimmy Carter, the President of the United States, asking him to stop sending military aid to El Salvador because it was used for violence and the oppression of his people.

In his regular radio broadcast on March 23, 1980, he called on the soldiers in the El Salvador military to refuse to obey the orders of their officers and stop killing their brothers and sisters. The very next day he was assassinated while conducting mass in the chapel of the hospital where he lived.

The identity of the assassin was no secret. He had been trained at the United States Army School of the Americas located at Fort Benning, Georgia. The assassin has never been arrested or charged for this crime. Obviously Bishop Romero was a threat to the domination system beyond the boundaries of El Salvador. As a candidate running for the presidency of the United States, Ronald Reagan had accused Jimmy Carter of having "lost" Nicaragua in 1979. With Nicaragua already claiming its independence from U.S. domination, the power systems in Washington, D.C. were not going to let El Salvador slip away. Bishop Romero had to be taken out.

Death does not have the last word. Life has the last word. As we have seen, Romero was not the first martyr (a word that means "witness") to be killed for challenging the Powers. Romero was not the last martyr either. Most of them are *el pueblo* themselves who choose life and fearlessly refuse to cooperate with their own death.

There are many people who still find inspiration in this faithful witness of Oscar Romero and his participation with *el pueblo*. Following the admonitions of Jesus, he became a political activist. The people I lived and worked with in Nicaragua view Bishop Romero as a true saint. So do I!

During this era hundreds of delegations from many countries went to Central America. Many went there to "help the poor" but had their attention turned to the *Power Line*. It was easy to see the source of the violence which came from Powers and domination systems. They were also able to observe the incredible power of *el pueblo* who are rich in the values we profess to hold most dear: hope, courage, respect, humility, generosity, loving kindness, sacrifice, and a commitment to pursue freedom even to the point of giving their lives for their neighbors.

When the musical group, *Peter, Paul and Mary*, came to Managua in July 1986, it was my genuine privilege to spend some time with them on two different occasions. They brought humanitarian aid for children in hospitals and were interested in knowing what the reality was for the people of Nicaragua. As they were preparing to leave, Mary shared a brief comment with me. She told me that Paul, who is a "born-again Christian", had been "reborn again." She said that Paul felt as though he had been "heart washed" in Nicaragua (as opposed to being brainwashed). Many of us who participated with the people of Nicaragua could report a similar experience.

Many members of these delegations learned for the first time about the policies of the United States that included *Low Intensity Conflict Warfare*. The leaders of the U.S. government did not want another Vietnam on their hands. They developed an official strategy called *Low Intensity Conflict Warfare*. It is a model of warfare designed to maintain U.S. dominance over Latin America and any other "trouble spots" in the world. The reference to *low intensity* simply means that it is low intensity for the citizens of the United States who can go on living as through they are not in engaged in any war at all. For the citizens of Nicaragua and other parts of Central America it resulted in high-intensity suffering.

When they were able to get on his schedule, delegations asked to meet with Father Miguel d'Escoto, the Foreign Minister of Nicaragua. I was present for several of these very informative conversations between Fr. d'Escoto and delegations from the United States. On one occasion one of the visitors asked Fr. d'Escoto how he, a priest, could continue to work with those "Communist Atheists" who, he had been told, were in control of the government of Nicaragua. Fr. d'Escoto responded by making reference to the Biblical story of the Good Samaritan.

He reviewed the story of the Good Samaritan, which continues the narrative at the beginning of this chapter. The story of Jesus and the scholar is expanded when the scholar attempts to justify himself by asking Jesus, "Who is my neighbor?" Jesus replied,

> "There was a man going from Jerusalem down to Jericho when he fell into the hands of robbers. They stripped him, beat him up, and went off, leaving him half dead. Now by coincidence a priest was going down that road; when he caught sight of the injured man he went out of his way to avoid him. In the same way, when a Levite came to the place, he took one look at him and crossed the road to avoid him. But this Samaritan who was traveling that way came to where he was and was moved to pity at the sight of him. He went up to him and bandaged his wounds, pouring olive oil and wine on them. He hoisted him onto his own animal, brought him to an inn, and looked after him. The next day he took out two silver coins, which he gave to the innkeeper, and said, "Look after him, and on my way back I'll reimburse you for any extra expense you have had."
>
> Then, according to the writer of Luke, Jesus asked the scholar, "Which of these three, do you think, acted like a neighbor to the man who fell into the hands of the robbers?" The scholar replied, "The one who showed him mercy." Jesus said, "Go and do likewise."

Miguel d'Escoto explained that the Jewish people of that time viewed the Samaritans with disdain and basically considered them to be "atheists." So, in response to the question about how he, as a Christian, could work with those "communist atheists," Fr. D'Escoto simply remarked, "We need more atheists like that." Fr. d'Escoto is making the point that his Sandinista brothers and sisters were engaged in the struggle for justice, which is more important than religious doctrine or law.

Most legal systems are designed to secure the interests of the wealthy and powerful. Jesus demonstrated that adherence to the law is only valid where the law itself served the interests of the poor and the disenfranchised. In this story of the Good Samaritan it was the laws related to cleanliness that prevented the priest and the Levite from getting involved with the man who had been beaten and left to die. By making the Samaritan the one who showed mercy the story addressed both religious and political issues. It was a reminder that God calls for justice, not doctrinal purity.

After discovering more truth about what was happening in Nicaragua many participants in the delegations returned home to challenge the policies of the United States. Even with the best of intentions most of these people weakened in their desire to change the systems. Although we may have some clear understanding that our foreign policy needs to be challenged, the fact is that in our daily lives we cooperate with the systems of power and privilege at many other levels. It is hard to effect change in systems that we depend upon for our own welfare or status!

Often fear takes over, and then the safe way to express the concern for others takes on the form of charity and benevolence. The church often mistakes benevolence for mission. Sending money is easier than risking the loss of our status and privilege. Jesus understood the dilemma we face all too well when he said we cannot serve two masters, i.e., we can't serve both God and Mammon (wealth). Jesus knows that the "affluent life" is a huge temptation, and he offers an alternative called the "abundant life."

The "affluent life" lends itself to charity and benevolence. The "abundant life" is what I observed as incarnate in *el pueblo*: hope, courage, respect, humility, generosity, loving kindness, sacrifice, and commitment to the point of giving their lives for their neighbors.

It is not easy to be the re-insurrection body of Christ. The cost of discipleship seems far too great. The Biblical theme of liberation calls us to expend the full extent of our energy and *agape* in the political task of creating the reign of God on this earth. It seems that as a society we prefer to adopt Salvation Theology and personalize our religion in the hope that we may go to heaven when we die. Salvation Theology does not require us to be martyrs. The illusion that just being a good person and an honest citizen sufficiently satisfies the ethical standards we have adopted from the mind of the oppressor. And, of course, let us remember to help those who are less fortunate.

Perhaps we don't view God as a full participant in the liberating process because we don't personally feel the need for liberation. Power and privilege seduce us. We have already mentioned the wisdom of Bishop Casaldaliga of Brazil, who says that once we have been to the university or the seminary we can never be one of *el pueblo* again.

In 1984 I felt called to live in voluntary poverty. I went to participate with those at the base. I was not going there to fix things for them, to educate them, to heal them or to save their souls. Many of my friends were quick to point out that I would never be able to truly be one of the poor. Nevertheless, I still felt the call to go to Nicaragua and learn what I could about the Christian Base Communities and the Sandinista Revolution. I have seen amazing power in the people when they have a vision of creating a society where life with dignity and peace with justice are the goals. Getting to know persons who have given their lives to this vision has also given me a glimpse of the vision as well.

There have been attempts to establish Christian Base Communities in the United States. These efforts have not met with much success. Liberation theology comes from those who live at the socio/economic base, and in this, the richest nation on earth, most of us do not live at the base. Even those who live in poverty in the United States may have options that most of the poor in Latin America have never known.

When Salvation Theology is offered to the poor it offers an escape from the misery of this world rather than an invitation to struggle. It calls for submission rather than resistance. But, the poor who respond to the Biblical theme of liberation do not look for charity from the Powers. They seek justice.

Indigenous people have paid a great price for those times when they have been unwilling to cooperate with their own oppression. Jesus qualifies as an "indigenous" person. His origins were deep in the traditions of the Jewish people. He not only suffered from the occupation of his homeland by a foreign power, but saw that the intrusion of Western philosophy and religion were part of the domination process. He also saw that those who had political and religious authority in his homeland allowed themselves to be co-opted by the domination systems because it benefited them to do so. In reading the story of Jesus, we should be clear that he was the leader of an indigenous struggle against the domination of a foreign empire and at the same time was engaged in attempting to call his own national leadership to be faithful to the God of their ancestors.

Involvement in the Politics of Liberation and Freedom requires a lot of volunteer time and energy. It is important to find a way to organize our participation so that it shifts from doing volunteer activity which supports the agenda of the

Powers to truly engaging activities that represent a challenge to the systems of domination and injustice. We will be more effective in our endeavor to participate with our neighbors who suffer from unjust systems if we begin to perceive our involvement as that of activists, political activists.

Martin Luther King, Jr's strategy of non-violent direct action represents one of the few illustrations we have in recent U.S. history that suggest that well-organized political strategies of non-violence can truly challenge the Powers and the status quo. He would have been less of a threat to the domination systems if he had limited his actions to the realm of ethics and morality based on religious persuasion. It is one of the few examples we have that reveals how faith in Jesus involves engagement in political struggle. Although these historic challenges to racism led to some changes in the laws related to civil rights it has not put an end to the struggle for civil rights in the United States.

Martin Luther King, Jr. understood that the challenge went beyond moral persuasion related to civil rights. He initiated political action to challenge economic structures that oppressed people. When he challenged the legitimacy of the war in Vietnam he struck at the heart of the control enjoyed by the Powers and the Military-Industrial Complex. This coalition of government, military and corporate power dominated the political and governmental structures of our society.

The civil rights movement was not about charity or an attempt to "help" the poor. Thousands of volunteers showed up to participate with those who suffered from systemic injustice. Without this kind of political activism and commitment to non-violence the movement would not have succeeded in its goal of systemic change.

Both Bishop Romero and Martin Luther King, Jr. were examples of how *agape* casts out fear. In both cases a broad-based struggle was set in motion to change the structures of evil systems with the intention of creating a more just society. These men engaged in non-violent political activism designed to challenge the Powers. It cost them their lives.

As difficult as it seems to share *agape* with those we consider to be our neighbor, we must also extend *agape* to our enemy. The creation of a more just society is not only to free prisoners, it is also a way of setting the jailer free. The goal includes the freeing of those who are the powerful from bondage to the domination systems of their own creation. In the process of engaging in the struggle, the methodology of non-violent *agape* is essential to free the oppressors from their own fear that *el pueblo* will express the same kind of violence to them that they have been using to dominate *el pueblo*.

Many of my friends are quick to point out that there is a great deal of "good" that has been done through charity and volunteerism. I agree that we should continue to engage in acts of kindness as a way of expressing love of neighbor. But we must ask ourselves about our motivation for doing so and whether our action represents anything other than our cooperation with the systems of domination.

A few days before Jesus was arrested by the temple guards he was with his disciples, at the home of Simon the leper. According to the story, a woman came up to him with an alabaster jar of very expensive ointment, and she poured it on his head as he sat at the table. When the disciples saw her do this they were very angry and said, "Why this waste? For this ointment could have been sold for a large sum, and the money given to the poor." But Jesus said to them, "Why do you trouble this woman? She has performed a good service for me. For you always have the poor with you, but you will not always have me."

Consistent with the mind of the oppressor, some people have used this scriptural reference, which says that "the poor will always be with us," as a basis on which to accept poverty and injustice as part of the status quo. However, I am convinced that what Jesus was actually saying was that the struggle goes on and the need to challenge systemic evil does not end.

The Kingdom of God is not accomplished in one great victory over the systems of domination. When Jesus went to the cross he understood that this action by itself would not eliminate the oppression of his people. However, he firmly believed that the ongoing expression of non-violent *agape* was the key to achieving a society of justice.

Jesus gave us the model. We can be grateful that the early followers got the message and engaged in the re-insurrection. We are not being asked to do the impossible. What was possible for those early followers is also possible for us.

The creation of the Kingdom of God is a process which, at the very least, involves finding ways to love our neighbor.

La lucha sigue…the struggle continues. Charity is not the way.

6

What About the Church?

Most people are of the opinion that the Christian Church was initiated by Jesus through the formation of his small band of disciples, but that is not the case. I can't emphasize it enough when I say, *Jesus did not set out to create a church.*

I have already reviewed how the development of the Christian Church emerged from the missionary endeavors of Paul as he promoted the idea among both Jews and Gentiles that Jesus was the hoped-for Messiah, the Christ. Due to the ease of travel in the Roman Empire, the previous dispersion of Jews throughout the Mediterranean world and the common use of the Greek language, the new "Christian" religion grew and the structures of the early Christian Church began to take shape. Paul's goal was to keep things stable and to get ready for the return of Jesus, which he believed was going to be very soon.

Paul could not have envisioned the ongoing development of the institution of the church as it took shape over the next several centuries. Although Christianity became the official religion of the Roman Empire, Paul would have been one of the first to recognize that the Emperor Constantine was not converted to Christianity so much as Christianity was utilized to serve the interests of the Roman Empire.

A basic reading of the history of Western Civilization reveals that instead of challenging the systemic evil of the domination systems, the Christian Church accepted its role as one of the Powers and continues in the present day to hold fast to its position of privilege and influence.

This was still the status of the Christian Church when I was baptized by my Grandfather. I was nine years old when I became a member of the West Side Methodist Church in Great Falls, Montana. Part of my formation as a Christian continued as I attended church camps when I was a youth in the mid-1940's. I always came away from those times at camp feeling motivated to be a better person.

In the 1960's I was a pastor in a small rural church in Montana. I always tried to take as many youth to camp as I could round up, and often served as the Dean of the Camp Staff. One evening during one of the camps we were sitting around the campfire listening to one of the pastors on our camping staff share his reflections on a book entitled, *God's Frozen People,* by T. Ralph Morton, a pastor, and Mark Gibbs, a lay person. The book made the point that the early followers of Jesus never participated in anything resembling what the Christian Church has become over these last 20 centuries:

- They never conceived of the church as a building.

- They never knew anything about Bishops or pastors who function as the head of churches or denominations.

- They never knew anything about seminaries that teach the doctrines to be handed down to the people in the churches.

- They never understood themselves as attaining social respectability by going to church.

Each of these images is a relatively accurate reflection of what came to my mind when mention was made in reference to the "church." Being socially respectable was definitely part of what it meant "to go to church." Respectability is still very central in the value system of my family and community. Certainly, in the role of a pastor and as a professor in a school of theology, I was expected to model social respectability.

I was impressed by the message I heard at the campfire. After I returned home to my small Montana community I ordered copies of the book with the intention of offering it to the members of my congregation as a study book. However, when I actually read the book for myself I discovered that the content was more radical than the limited images shared around the campfire at church camp. The authors wrote their message in prophetic and challenging language about the failure of the church to be more engaged in the struggle for social justice. While I agreed with much of what they had to say, at the same time the message of the book caused me to feel very apprehensive.

In the end, I never found the courage to offer the book to my congregation. After months of indecision I returned the books. My rationalization for not initiating a study of this book was that the material was too radical for the members of the congregation. Obviously, I had projected my own fear on the congregation by determining that it was *"they"* who were not ready for this challenging message.

I was afraid that by introducing *God's Frozen People* I might create more conflict in the congregation. It was the time of the Civil Rights struggle and other social upheaval. Many members of the congregation were conservative in their approach to both politics and religion. Just preaching from the Revised Standard Version of the Bible rather than the King James Version was enough to come under the suspicion of being a communist. I felt particularly vulnerable because the chairperson of the Official Board of the church was also the head of *The John Birch Society,* a radical right-wing organization. I had already had some encounters on a number of social issues with this lay person and wasn't ready to challenge him any further.

Introducing conflict into a congregation is not the best way to move up the ladder of success in the ministry. So it was very early in my ministry I learned that there is safety in sticking with the Biblical theme of salvation. I really do understand when pastors step back from the prophetic passages of the Bible which focus on the struggle for justice. I did it myself.

When I am in a conversation with another person I bring my Credo with me because, in a real sense, my Credo is me. Although I didn't know how to name my experience in those early years of ministry, I was engaged in a Credo-to-Credo process. Each person with whom I have a conversation brings his or her Credo to the dialogue. I know that much of my apprehension about sharing the material in the book, which at that time seemed so radical, was because I did not have a clear sense of my own Credo with which to engage in dialogue with the authors. It also meant I did not have a clear sense of my own Credo from which to engage in dialogue with the congregation. I can see now that my ministry was based on a great deal of dependence on outside sources, including a sense of what the congregation would accept or reject.

What I have identified as the Biblical theme of salvation was at that time and continues to be the prevailing approach to understanding Christianity in our society. For instance, in Bill Moyer's documentary, *God and Politics: The Kingdom Divided,* a young woman expressed an important part of her Credo when she said, "It is better to save your soul and go to heaven, than to save the world and go to hell." Her comment is focused on personal redemption and her hope for eternal life. The comment also reflects a critical attitude toward those who place an emphasis on matters of social justice. Although the statement is brief, it illustrates much of the tension in the religious sector of our society today.

The Biblical theme of salvation is constantly in front of us in our culture. When people think of the meaning of Christianity that is what comes to mind. For the most part, people I visit with say they have not been introduced to the

Biblical theme of liberation. I have developed a listing to identify the tensions and tendencies that these two Biblical themes embody. People with whom I have shared this listing say that they found it helpful in thinking through their own understanding of faith and the role of the Church.

Biblical Theme of Salvation	**_Biblical Theme of Liberation_**
Influence of Paul	Influence of Jesus
Western philosophy	Hebrew or Middle-Eastern philosophy
Separation of religion & politics	Integration of religion and politics
Greater focus on religion	Greater focus on politics
Cross seen as a religious symbol	Cross seen as a tool of political violence
Mind of Christ (Epistles)	Mind of Jesus (First three Gospels)
God in Heaven	God as a full participant in the struggle
Future orientation—Second Coming	Present orientation—freedom now
Christ as Son of God (Savior)	Jesus as Son of Man (Liberator)
Crucifixion required for atonement	No atonement required
Immortality-life after death	Living with freedom and justice on earth
Church	Kingdom of God
Control of the Means of Grace	Grace Happens
Power over	Power with
Allegiance to the Church	Allegiance to God
Concerned with personal sin	Concerned with systemic evil
Concerned with right doctrine	Concerned with right action
Pastoral care	Prophetic vision
Emphasis on the Law	Emphasis on Justice
Acceptance of violence	Non-Violence
Just War	No War
Mission as Evangelism	Mission as Participation
Motivated by saving souls	Motivated by saving lives
Charity (doing "to & for")	Kindness (doing "with")

Biblical Theme of Salvation	**Biblical Theme of Liberation**
Volunteer (focus on "*poverty line*")	Activist (focus on "*power line*")
Fearful—seeking security	Fearless—taking risks

Working through the tensions that exist between these themes has helped me be clearer about my Credo. For instance, I had to deal at length with the tension between violence or non-violence as part of my Credo. Most of my life I have expressed support for the concept of non-violence and respected those who believed in it. I actively supported the right of people to take the position of being a conscientious objector to military service, but made the choice to serve in the military myself. At the time I saw no conflict of faith in my actions. Valuing the concept of non-violence and making a commitment to live in a way that is truly non-violent are very different things. Non-violence did not become a firm commitment of faith and life for me until these last fifteen years.

The point is that we evolve and grow in our faith. Our Credo reflects the choices we have made along our spiritual and political journey. Contrasting and comparing these Biblical themes of Salvation and Liberation can lend more depth to our faith and substance to our beliefs.

In the Introduction I used part of the Sermon on the Mount where Jesus said, "Enter through the narrow gate; for the gate is wide and the road is easy that leads to destruction, and there are many who take it. For the gate is narrow and the road is hard that leads to life, and there are few who find it." Reflecting on these two Biblical themes may help us to see which road or gate we have taken in our lives.

Jesus could have saved himself from being arrested, tortured and crucified by submitting to the authority of Rome and the Jewish authorities. The choice Jesus made as he prayed in the Garden of Gethsemane has echoed down through history, "Not my will, but thy will be done." He trusted that God's love has greater power than the violence of the Powers. He stayed true to his belief that *non-violence* and *agape* are necessary to realize God's will in the struggle for peace and justice.

We choose the wide gate and the easy road that leads to destruction when we cooperate with the Politics of Power and Domination, which also, involves the Methodology of Violence. With few exceptions in its long history, Christendom has aided in promoting the illusion or myth of "redemptive violence." By focusing on the tensions and tendencies between these two Biblical themes we can explore ways to make a faithful response to the God who is with us in the midst of our personal and corporate lives. Exploring these tensions may aid others, as it has me, to recognize that we have choices to make and they are not always easy choices.

Jesus understood that the religion of his forefathers and mothers had failed to be a force for true freedom and justice. He had a word to say to the authorities of his own religion. He called them hypocrites. In other words they lacked the integrity of being true to the moral and religious beliefs they professed.

Every president of the United States who has held office in my lifetime has operated from the Politics of Power and Domination. Each has promoted volunteerism and charity in one form or another as a way of dealing with poverty and social concerns. Each of them has engaged in acts of war in the name of "national defense" and promised to maintain our position of dominance in this world while at the same time invoking the blessing of God on our nation. Being the Chief Executive Officer and Commander in Chief of the most powerful nation in the world lends itself to arrogance and deceit. Hypocrisy does not seem to be a problem for those who are in positions of power and authority. We are continually being deceived by our political and religious leaders.

I can think of no better example of hypocrisy than that which we observe in the actions taken by George W. Bush, who is presently the resident of the White House. President Bush has promoted a faith-based initiative for social programs and at the same time initiated a preemptive war based on duplicity and fraud. Engaging in this kind of pseudo-compassion, while also engaging in messianic militarism is an abomination.

To engage in these actions and at the same time proclaim that he is doing these things under the guidance of God should be met with outrage rather than being praised by Christians. Truth is one of the first victims of war and I am concerned that during this Bush Administration the boundaries of executive power and secrecy have extended far beyond that of those who previously sat in the Oval Office.

When we call ourselves "Christians" and still cooperate fully with the illusion that through violence we can achieve peace, and that through acts of charity we can achieve social justice, are we not equally open to the charge of hypocrisy? Are we any less blameworthy? Christian Church leaders have become skilled at the diversion of adopting moralistic resolutions and then continuing to cooperate with the Politics of Power and Domination.

In his book, *Moral Man and Immoral Society: A Study of Ethics and Politics*, Reinhold Neibuhr was addressing the issues of social responsibility in a time of social upheaval in the 1930's. He contends that it is possible for an individual person to be moral because each individual has a conscience and is able to make a moral choice even to the point of giving his or her life for a friend. Neibuhr is not saying that every person makes good moral choices, but that it is a possibility.

On the other hand Neibuhr states that social organizations like labor unions, corporations and nation states, which are formed around self-interest, cannot be moral because they have no conscience. With the greatest of sincerity he raises the question about whether the Church, as an institution, can be moral or whether it is like other organizations formed around self-interest. By raising this question Neibuhr was challenging the hypocrisy of the Church, which seems all too ready to preach, "Peace, Peace…" when there is no peace. So, what about the Church? Does being a member of the Christian Church represent a choice to take the wide road or the narrow gate?

While I was on the faculty of Saint Paul School of Theology, Anne Wilson Schaef was invited as a guest lecturer and at the same time conducted a seminar for the faculty on sexism. One observation she made was that the Church has been assigned the "female role" in our society. As such, the Church's role is to promote religion, teach morality and engage in serving and taking care of others. On the other hand, Anne observed that the realm of politics is assigned to the "male role," which deals with making the major decisions about economics, structures of government, foreign policy, matters of national defense, engaging in war, etc.

I have found Anne's ability to keep things simple has also made it easier for me keep things in perspective. However, what follows here, in drawing on her insight, should be attributed to me and not to her.

On those occasions when clergy and lay leaders attempt to challenge the Politics of Power and Domination they are risking repercussions for crossing an invisible barrier and entering the forbidden domain of the "male role." While such endeavors may engage the ire of the Powers, it is just as likely that church leaders who engage in political actions will be taken to task by their own church members who also operate from the mind of the oppressor. The usual penalty for breaking this political barrier is the withdrawal of financial support or a move to another church that does not challenge the domination system and may even support male dominance as a doctrine.

In the Chapter on Love of Neighbor we have already seen the consequences that resulted from the intervention into the domain of the "male role" by Bishop Romero and Martin Luther King, Jr. The lives of these two men are powerful examples of removing the blinders of Salvation Theology and recognizing that Jesus never saw any separation of religion and politics. Jesus was active in challenging the authorities, including the systemic evil of male dominance. To assign Jesus and his mission to the realm of religion is a way to de-politicize his life. Strangely, even to identify Jesus as the Son of God, or as the Christ, is enough to establish his role as primarily that of a religious figure and remove his influence from the domain of politics.

Throughout this book I have been encouraging the link between religion and politics. Political involvement by some religious sectors of the society in the hot issues of abortion and gay marriage illustrate serious attempts to utilize the governing structures for the promotion of a particular doctrinal stance. However, rather than challenging the Powers and domination systems these religious agendas are examples of combining forces with the Politics of Power and Domination. It is a game of mutual manipulation where the self-interest of each group derives benefits from the process. Remembering how Constantine co-opted the early Christian Church in service to the Roman Empire, I believe the current Powers and domination systems have co-opted the Christian Churches. Now, as then, the true mission of Jesus gets lost in the process.

Egun Mehmet Caner and Emir Fethi Caner, two former Muslims who are now evangelical professors, explore the question of "Just War Theory" and examine the history of Christians killing in the name of God. In their book entitled, *Christian Jihad,* they propose a central premise that guides the study of Church history. They say that whenever the church and the state enter into a relationship, inevitably the church ends up becoming the state's whore. She is used for the political expedience of the state, and when she is no longer useful, she is tossed aside as an unwanted mistress. It is an unholy relationship, and the state is inevitably an abusive spouse.

Today, Jesus would be just as ready to challenge the hypocrisy of those who profess to represent his values by calling themselves "Christians" while cooperating fully with oppressive systems. Jesus' call for integrity in political and religious action is still relevant. His own integrity was established, not through cooperation with the Powers, but by challenging them.

For the academic year of 1966–67 I was a Fellow in the Division of Religion and Psychiatry at the Menninger Foundation in Topeka, Kansas. One of the projects I worked on at the time had to do with how campus ministers in Kansas understand the role of the church in society. One particular interview resulted in an image of the church that is both an observation of reality, and at the same time offers a challenge. As follows:

He suggests that we use a factory that manufactures grease and lubricants as a metaphor to describe the Church. Visitors who come to the plant are given a tour of the facilities. Everything seems up to date and the workers in the plant seem to be content in doing their assigned tasks. The plant is impressive and seems very productive.

During the tour the guide makes it clear that it is a growing business and that they are looking for more people to work in the plant. There are many opportunities available if the visitors want to apply. When the tour is finished the guide then asks if there are any questions.

One of the visitors made an observation that during the entire tour they had not seen the loading docks where they shipped out their lubrication products. The tour guide said it was a good observation, because there are no shipping docks.

The explanation was that, *they need to use all of the grease and lubricants manufactured in the factory just to keep the factory working.*

In the world of business this would be an apt description of a failed project. It is no less true if it fits for the church. Many churches have even adopted the language of the business world when we say that we are about the task of "growing" the church. For some, the church has become big business, and for others, a source of entertainment. What the Church has not become is the *re-insurrection body of Christ.*

A comment of a friend who is not a church member was, "Surely the church has done some good." His comment is consistent with the notion that the role of the church in society is just that, "to do good." In many church settings a great deal of loving-kindness is shared and genuine efforts are given to build a community of support for one another. Often people find the care and support they desire in the church setting that they may not find in other social settings. This is good, but unfortunately many churches are content to settle for simply nurturing their own members and promoting their own growth.

Regrettably, some people report the experience of being the object of judgment and condemnation on the part of other members of the congregations in which they participate. Anyone who has been a participant in a congregation knows that conflicts abound, resentments are held, competition exists, class differences are noted, etc. In other words, the Church is a gathering of imperfect human beings. It is not a perfect organization and for those who have eyes to see, hypocrisy abounds. Perhaps we should put signs in front of our churches that read, "*Sinners-'R-Us.*"

Loving those who love us in return is not the point. Judging others is not the way to construct the reign of God. Competition between and amongst churches and denominations, especially as it is based on doctrinal differences, only illustrates the fractured nature of the Church. There is no light here; only darkness.

I am part of that conflicted social experiment we call the Church; in my case, the United Methodist Church. I genuinely value our Wesleyan Heritage and have seen some members of my denomination engage in an attemmpt to build a better society. However, I am also disappointed much of the time. For instance, I have seen my denomination expend most of its energy during the last four decades fighting over the doctrinal issues related to homosexuality. For some, the pain of the conflict has come to the point of splitting the church. There are forces within our ranks who promote their version of doctrinal purity to the point that I want to ask, "Where's the focus on love and justice?" All of this is done under the heading of claiming to have the true vision of Christ and the true vision of what the Church is called to be and do…and Jesus gets lost in the shuffle.

Years ago I had a friend who was a radical preacher. He was radical in calling for justice. Someone challenged his approach by saying, "If you keep on preaching like this, you will split the church." He responded by saying, "Okay. Let's split her open and see what she's made of." I ponder about why it is that "doctrinal purity" seems to get in the way of seeking justice or even doing basic acts of kindness, which is the point of the Biblical story of the Good Samaritan. Why is it that doctrinal purity seems to introduce fear when justice calls for love? Why is it that speaking truth to powers introduces conflict in the church? Maybe, just maybe, after 40 years in the wilderness of struggling with homosexuality, it is time to split the church open and see what it is made of.

While I was living in Nicaragua I had the opportunity to participate with a group called the Ecumenical Committee. The participants were internationalists, although most were from the United States. They represented a wide range of religious backgrounds, including United Methodists, Presbyterians, Roman Catholics, Mennonites, Quakers, Lutherans, Seventh Day Adventists, Baptists, Buddhists, members of the United Church of Canada, participants in Witness for Peace, and others.

Our purpose was to identify and engage in political action as it related to matters of injustice. Each of us brought our own church traditions and beliefs with us. However, as we focused on promoting justice we simply put our doctrinal differences on the side of the table. We were linked by one common thread embedded in each of our traditions because each of our participants felt that being faithful meant to work for peace. In the context of the war in Nicaragua it was obvious to all of us that there could be no peace without justice.

Was that the Church I was a part of in that setting? For me, at least it lent a ray of hope for the Church. Even though most of us had gone there with the desire to be engaged in the mission of the Church, the truth is that we received much more than we gave. The Christian Base Communities and *La Insurrección Evangelica* inspired all of us.

I am very grateful for the opportunity I had to participate with *el pueblo* in Nicaragua as they openly demonstrated their belief in a God who is a full participant in their struggle for freedom and justice. They believed that not only could they challenge the Powers; they could challenge the "Super Powers."

The members of the Christian Base Communities in Nicaragua amazed me with their devotion to their Church. They never wavered from their commitment to the Roman Catholic Church, even when it was obvious to them that the hierarchy of their church was cooperating with the policies of the United States. The liberation theme they found in reading the Bible also led them to engage in efforts to change their church and turn it around from its long history of domination and participating in the oppression of *el pueblo*. These people not only believed that in the struggle between the rich and the poor the Church should make a preferential option for the poor…these people are the poor and they clearly saw their role as promoting justice and creating the Kingdom of God.

When I first arrived in Nicaragua in 1984, I lived with a family in Esteli while studying Spanish. At that time they had lost two sons in the war with the U.S. sponsored Contra, two of their daughters were in the Nicaraguan Army, and two young children were still at home. During one of the most difficult times of the struggle, in 1988, I had a chance to visit with them. With inflation running rampant the family was more economically distressed than ever before. I asked Guillermo, my Nicaraguan father, what he saw in the future given the hardships with which they were continuously faced. He said, "*First, you must remember that we are a people of hope. And second, justice is on our side.*" As members of the Christian Base Community movement they always reflected on their life situation from a perspective of faith which had justice at its heart. They also had a long view of the struggle.

I was reminded of something written by Rubem Alves, a Latin American proponent of Liberation Theology. He wrote, "Let us plant dates even though those who plant them will never eat them. We must live by the love of what we well never see. Such disciplined love is what has given prophets, revolutionaries, and saints the courage to die for the future they envisage. They make their own bodies the seed of their highest hope." I saw that hope incarnated in the life of *el pueblo* in Nicaragua. I observed hope where there was no apparent reason for hope.

During the mid-1980's thousands of young men and women were dying in the jungles and mountains of Nicaragua. It was clear that the Contras were a mercenary force under the control of the C.I.A.. It was also obvious that Cardinal Obando y Bravo was the most powerful political force in Nicaragua who stood in opposition to the Sandinista Revolution and Liberation Theology.

An organization called *The Mothers of Martyrs and Heroes of the Revolution* emerged during this time of warfare. Each week a group of 8-10 of these women would go to the office of the Cardinal seeking an "audience" with him. The composition of the group from one week to another involved different women, but they would not let a week go by without attempting a meeting with the Cardinal. The women had a simple request for their meeting with the Cardinal. It was the same each week. They wanted him to offer a prayer at Mass for their loved ones who had died in the war with the Contras. He knew why they were there and yet he refused to meet with them. Still, every week, these women would go to his office and sit quietly, waiting to see the Cardinal. He never held an audience with them. It seems that for these women, a combination of forgiveness and perseverance was at the heart of loving the Church rather than leaving the Church.

Perhaps it was the martyrdom of many priests and lay leaders that still permitted them to stay true to a church that denied them spiritual support in the midst of their pain. Bishop Romero, who participated with *el pueblo* in El Salvador, had become a Saint in the eyes of these women. They remembered Bishop Casaldaliga from Brazil and his trips to Nicaragua to encourage them in support of *La Insurrección Evangelica*, the non-violent Gospel Insurrection.

Santos, my Nicaraguan mother, was one of those who sat in vigil in the office of the Cardinal; to no avail. When *el pueblo* speak their truth to power we get a glimpse of the integrity that comes from knowing that God is a participant in their lives. These Mothers of Martyrs and Heroes were women of integrity. I can't say that for the hierarchy of the Roman Catholic Church in Nicaragua.

Almost fifty years ago, when I was still a seminary student, one of my Church History professors said, "Jesus preached the coming of the Kingdom of God, but what we got was the Church." At the time, I didn't understand the deeper meaning of what he had to say. Now, it is clear to me that there is a huge disparity between what Jesus set out to accomplish and the subsequent development of a new religion and an institution called the Christian Church.

In regard to the goals that Jesus set forth, the Church would appear to be a failed project. Insofar as the Church claims to be the "Body of Christ" here again, the Church would seem to have failed in that mission. There is presently a great deal of talk about Church renewal. While that is a very desirable thing to contemplate, I am quite sure that the Church will continue to be a failed project if our energy is simply focused on the renewal of the church. It is very difficult for me to see the possibility that God can use this very imperfect institution we call the Church to bring about a more just society if it continues to cooperate with the Politics of Power and Domination.

To focus on the renewal of the church will only continue to use all our strength to keep the church running and have no visible loading dock where the well intentioned purposes for being the Church can be exported to the world.

Our focus must be on what Jesus had in mind, which is the creation of the Kingdom of God. The pursuit of this vision requires us to become political activists by engaging in the Politics of Liberation and Freedom. By doing this we may see some renewal of the Church, but that is not the goal. If renewal happens, it will be a gift of grace.

Somehow, by the grace of God, this imperfect instrument called the Church managed to keep the story of Jesus from drifting into obscurity and being lost forever. For that I am grateful. Even then, I never really understood the story until I was given a whole new understanding of Jesus and his ministry by reading the scripture through the eyes of *el pueblo* and more importantly, seeing it incarnated in the lives of these humble people.

In working through the tensions and tendencies between the Biblical theme of Salvation and the Biblical theme of Liberation it would seem that there is a need to find some balance between them. Up to this point in history it has been almost entirely weighted toward the side of Salvation Theology. In some cases there may need to be a choice between one Biblical theme or the other. Mostly it is a matter of seeing that both are present in the Bible and that working on the creative tensions they present will lend to a more abundant life of faith.

To be concerned about our personal sin does not need to stand in opposition to being concerned with systemic evil. In the same manner, to volunteer our energy in an act of kindness does not need to stand in opposition to being a political activist. Many believers are concerned about immortality or life after death. Does the focus on Salvation need to be in tension with believers who want to live in the pursuit of freedom and justice while living on earth?

I believe that the post-crucifixion narratives shared by the first followers of Jesus illustrate their firm belief that there is life after death. The first participants in the Jesus Movement perceived that God's love, *agape,* is even stronger than death. It was also their discovery that the trust Jesus placed in non-violent *agape* is the method required to bring the Kingdom of God into being on this earth. For this small band of followers their post-crucifixion encounters with Jesus did not lead to a period of waiting for Jesus to return. Rather, they accepted the task of achieving their liberation and freedom themselves by utilizing Jesus' model.

If the mission of Jesus is to go forth it must be through the same experience for us that was true for his earliest followers. Jesus must win our hearts and minds. Those who began the Jesus Movement understood that with Jesus no longer a part of their human community the struggle for justice was left to them to accomplish. In the same way we must understand that it is now up to us.

At this point in history, Jesus has not come again to accomplish the hoped for "glorious banquet." In the meantime we must be willing to be the re-insurrection body of Christ. If not that, then why bother with the church?

Bill Moyers was on target when he understood that the primary theme of his documentary was about *God and Politics*. However his subtitle, *The Kingdom Divided*, was a little skewed. It was this little insignificant vessel of human endeavor we call the Church that was divided. The church is more divided now than when Moyers made the documentary. The Kingdom of God continues to wait for our willingness to bring it into being.

I believe that the Spirit of the living God who led Jesus into the wilderness and gave him a vision of the Kingdom of God is still participating with us today. Staying connected with the Spirit will help us stay focused on Jesus. Prayer is one of the ways to stay connected to the Spirit and to seek guidance about how to engage in living faithful lives.

So, what about the Church?

I will pray for the Church.

PART III
Credo to Credo: A Series of Interactive Dialogues

7

Credo to Credo: You, the Reader, and I

I was born in 1933 and lived a short distance from where the Sun River flowed out of the Rocky Mountains in Montana. We lived nearby my Grandfather, Rev. Leo E. Baldwin, who was a pioneer Methodist preacher. I was brought up in the tradition of John and Charles Wesley, a tradition which encouraged each person to engage in the task of articulating one's own theology. Briefly, the "Wesleyan Tradition" introduces a methodology for doing the theological task based on the integration of four subjects: The Bible, Tradition, Experience and Reason.

The development of my Credo began early in my life and was not deeply profound or complex. For example, I went to Sunday School with my older sister and brother, where I was taught a simple little song with these lyrics, "Jesus loves me, this I know, for the Bible tells me so." Note:

- It is a statement of faith when I say, "Jesus loves me."
- I state how I came to that belief when I say, "…the *Bible* tells me so."
- The song was consistent with Christian *Tradition*.
- I had the *Experience* of being loved in the process of learning the song.
- As a statement of belief it seemed *Reasonable* to myself and others.

Of course the issues of faith and life are vastly more complex than this little song. Expressing what I believe about God is a process of discovery as new levels of understanding about the Bible, tradition and my own experience take shape in and through reasoned expression and dialogue. Expressing my Credo is not simply an intellectual conclusion to which I come but an awareness that leads to other levels of truth that continue to change and develop.

For most people who profess to follow the teachings of Jesus, the Bible is given a place of predominance. Such was the case for Thomas Jefferson. In a letter written to John Adams in 1813, Jefferson reveals a unique approach to reading the Gospel. He wrote,

> "We must reduce our volume (the Bible) to the simple Evangelists; select, even from them, the very words only of Jesus, paring off the amphibologisms (ambiguities) into which they have been led, by forgetting often, or not understanding, what had fallen from Him, by giving their own misconceptions as his dicta, and expressing unintelligibly for others what they had not understood themselves. There will be found remaining the most sublime and benevolent code of morals which has ever been offered to man. I have performed this operation for my own use, by cutting verse out of the printed book, and arranging the matter which is evidently his and which is as easily distinguished as diamonds in a dunghill."

Jefferson brought his own experience and reason to the traditions which were prevalent at the time. He did not feel bound by the Canon of the New Testament, which was determined by the Bishops in the fourth century who destroyed and ignored a number of other writings with which they disagreed. Jefferson kept his focus on Jesus and did not adopt a literal approach to the reading of the Bible. In order to find his "diamonds" it was not necessary to make reference to the writings of Paul, the other epistles, or the book of Revelation.

Hundreds upon hundreds of highly qualified Biblical scholars have spent their lives trying to sort out the essence of the Scripture. Each new discovery of ancient documents always leads to another round of scholarly investigation. Just in my lifetime there have been volumes upon volumes of research and writing that attempt to describe the life of Jesus.

El pueblo in Nicaragua had no access to these massive resources. Nonetheless, they were able to identify basic truths revealed in the Scripture when they had a chance to read it in their own language and reflect on it for themselves. Perhaps these humble people had a less cluttered view of the message from where they lived at the base of the socio/economic pyramid. At the very least they discovered a God who participates in their suffering and who is a full participant in their struggle for freedom and justice.

. It is my sincere hope that you, the reader, will be motivated to reconsider your own Credo. Taking the constitutional right to freedom of religion seriously is the first step toward participating in the Politics of Liberation and Freedom.

8

Credo-to-Credo: Grandpa and I

My grandparents, Rev. and Mrs. Leo E. Baldwin, had eight children. In order to support the family they got into the bee business. I grew up seeing the label *Baldwin and Sons Beeline Honey,* which was also displayed in big bold letters on the front of the old green warehouse. Everyone in the Sun River Valley knew where it was. Until I was nine years old my childhood home was just a block away from Grandpa and Grandma.

During the summer the bees gathered the honey and in the early fall the harvest was a very busy time. This source of income allowed Grandpa to commit most of the time to his ministry and still provide for family members to attend school and go off to college. After Grandpa retired from the ministry he still worked with the bees. As summer employment during the last two years of my university education, 1953–1955, I worked with Grandpa to bring in the honey harvest.

I considered Grandpa to be pretty strict because he never worked on Sunday. We always had devotions in the morning and grace before meals. He didn't approve of dancing or card playing, which was probably more about using time for trivial pursuits than it was about sinful behavior. He was a serious scholar and very progressive for his day. He had a generous spirit and I never heard him stand in judgment of another person.

On one occasion I asked Grandpa a question. I have long since forgotten the reason for asking, but I inquired about what foods would be the minimum that a person would need to sustain life. Grandpa pondered the question for a few minutes. I needed to wait while he considered his best answer. If I was impatient it not only interfered with his thinking, but would also be disrespectful. When he answered me, he said that the minimum foods required to sustain life are bread and wine.

These were strange words coming from my Grandpa who had never taken a drink of alcohol in his life. No, not even wine, not even for communion! At the time, I didn't really understand his answer. However, he had truly given me his view of what is essential to maintain life. He had given me the essence of his Credo. Grandpa had a sacramental view of life. I have never forgotten his answer.

It wasn't until a few years ago that one of my uncles told me that Grandpa was one of the first members of the Methodist Federation for Social Action which was formed in the 1908. He was more involved in the struggle for social justice than I had observed or realized. Grandpa was a man of integrity. He was his Credo.

I often find myself in dialogue with what I remember of my Grandfather. For instance, Grandpa felt that people have a deep spiritual hunger and that all too often they participate in the life of the Church without getting any solid spiritual nourishment. I am convinced that his concern still holds true today. A steady diet of Salvation Theology is not spiritually nourishing. One needs to get a balanced diet and be introduced to the solid spiritual food found in the Biblical theme of liberation.

Of course there are issues about which Grandpa and I would have disagreements. My Christology certainly has taken some turns that I would like to discuss with him. Hopefully, he would see that I to have adopted a "sacramental view" of life and am growing in the faith.

9

Credo to Credo: Mel Gibson and I

Mel Gibson's movie, The *Passion of the Christ*, is an incredible way for him to present his Credo. He did a great deal of research over more than a decade before he released his Credo for all of us to see. This movie/credo generated an abundance of commentary and discussion.

Salvation is the central theme of the movie. Gibson begins with the premise that Jesus is the Son of God. He wants to visually show that Jesus stays true to a prophetic script, which had been written by the Prophet Isaiah and which was displayed for all of us to read on the large screen at the opening of the film. In this script the only way for Jesus to bear our sins was to go through suffering and agony and ultimately end up on the Cross.

Actually, in spite of all the conflicts that surrounded the release of this film, Gibson's stance of faith is not radical in any sense. It fits well within the orthodox tradition of the Christian Church handed down to us over the centuries. Passion Plays have been in existence for many centuries. However, in the very first scene in the movie, Gibson introduces us to a non-Biblical encounter between Jesus and Satan in the Garden of Gethsemane. Satan is trying to convince Jesus that no one can bear that heavy a burden. After this rather mysterious and foreboding beginning the violence begins and never lets up.

Mel Gibson stays within liturgical Christian tradition when he presents the "Passion" as the suffering Jesus endured following his arrest and continuing until his death on the Cross. As the director of his own film, Gibson does an artful job of taking us through the trials, the whipping, the scourging, the mocking, the carrying of the cross and the crucifixion. He wanted us to see the suffering. He wanted us to feel the violence and be emotionally involved. Through the use of Hollywood-style artistic license, special effects and varied music on the sound track viewers are kept on a disturbing roller coaster of feeling and shock.

By being so focused on the Biblical theme of salvation, Gibson seems to have entirely missed the political dimension which defined the life of Jesus and his nation. Indeed, it appears that he had no clue to the Biblical theme of liberation in which the passion of Jesus is not limited to the last hours before he died. The passion of Jesus begins with the fact that he was an indigenous person born to a people who had known the oppression of empires more than once in their history. For the Jewish people an understanding of God was shaped more by their political history than by their religious rituals. The prophets saw that God was not interested in their religious ceremonies so much as in the issues of justice. The Biblical theme of liberation requires a larger screen to see it.

Mel Gibson would have done well to think of Jesus in the same terms as the acting role he portrayed in the struggle of the Scottish patriot, William Wallace, in the movie, *Braveheart.* William Wallace was passionate about achieving freedom for his homeland. So was Jesus. William Wallace was crucified because he was leading an insurrection against the Powers and domination systems of his day. Jesus was also crucified because he was engaged in an insurrection against the Powers of his day.

The difference between the approach taken by William Wallace and that of Jesus was that Jesus knew violence would only lead to more violence. Jesus did not go to the cross to pay for the sins of humankind. Rather, Jesus went to the cross to prevent the continuing cycle of violence. Jesus' purpose in going to the cross was to model how the struggle for freedom can be won through non-violent *agape* with the full participation of God in the process.

Mel Gibson needs to recognize that there was no more need to introduce Satan into this movie about Jesus than there was a need to introduce Satan into the movie about William Wallace. There was plenty of evil to overcome with the Powers and domination systems whose violence was and is always in direct opposition to the passion for justice that God calls for through the voice of his prophets. Jesus was just such a prophet and his crime was not simply calling for justice, but for leading a movement to achieve justice.

Gibson essentially limited his Credo and the film to the last few hours that preceded the death of Jesus. Although he expanded his understanding of the life of Jesus through the use of a few flashbacks he did not capture the significance of the liberation movement that defined the activities of Jesus. Jesus did not go to the cross to satisfy some pre-ordained requirement set forth by an alienated God. This was not an action of martyrdom to ransom the sins of the world. The populist movement or insurgency initiated by Jesus ultimately led him to Jerusalem and the cross. This was not the living out of some predicted or pre-ordained script, it was a choice Jesus made. Jesus was very clear that his choice to reveal the power of non-violence came at a price.

Jesus was not killed as an innocent victim of a rather reluctant Pilate as depicted in the movie. Jesus was an insurrectionist. He was guilty, as charged. He was crucified because he represented a true political threat. He had challenged both the Jewish authorities and the Roman Empire with an insurrection, albeit a non-violent insurrection.

Mel Gibson captured the significance of the violence that comes forth from the Powers when they are challenged. However, Gibson misses the significance of non-violence as the major message of the Passion Play. He is not alone. Most Christians don't get it either.

The brief clip at the end of the film which shows a cleaned up visage of a very Italian-looking Christ shows that Gibson knows something of the importance of the resurrection in the story spelled out in the Scripture. However, Gibson has failed to recognize that without the rest of the story involving the re-insurrection there would not have been a legend about which he could make a movie. The only reason we have the story to tell is that the followers of Jesus continued the insurrection Jesus had begun. They were convinced that if the resurrection of Jesus had any meaning at all it was that we cannot serve two masters. We cannot submit to the authority of the domination systems and still serve God. Well, maybe this part of the story will be filmed some day as a sequel.

Mel Gibson's movie and the theology it engenders do not represent any threat to the Powers and domination systems of our own day. The opposite is true because it lends credibility to the theology of law and judgment, which under girds the religious institutions and churches that cooperate fully with the Politics of Power and Domination.

This movie does not represent the true passion of God expressed by the prophets and revealed in Jesus. It did not reflect the Politics of Liberation and Freedom, which has the Kingdom of God as the goal. Justice is achieved through non-violent resistance and struggle, not a pre-ordained sacrifice. The power of non-violent *agape* over violence is the message of the cross.

If Mel Gibson wants to invest in another movie I would encourage him to make a movie about the Politics of Liberation and Freedom where we can see the passion of Jesus as the true *Braveheart.*

10

Credo to Credo: Alice Walker and I

Alice Walker is one of *el pueblo* who found her voice. Through her writing she shares her Credo and it speaks volumes to those who have eyes to see and ears to hear. She has taken me on journeys to places I have never been and exposes me to a reality I have never known.

Alice Walker was the eighth child of sharecroppers in the State of Georgia. Due to a childhood accident she was blinded in one eye. She was the Valedictorian of her school and against the odds of our social structures went on to finish college. Her contributions and her gifts were recognized through the award of the Pulitzer Prize. She has the gift of telling the truth without being judgmental. There is no way to miss her passion for justice as she writes about the oppressive realities of racism, sexism, rape, female disfigurement and poverty. She reveals the deeper levels of what it means to be human and spiritual at the same time.

I, on the other hand, was born during the depression to hard-working parents. It was a hard life, but it was a good life. My parents had a small farm on which we had cows, chickens, rabbits, pigs, lots of flowers and a really huge garden. We lived in the Sun River Valley in Montana with the magnificent Rocky Mountains and their snow-covered peaks as our backdrop each day. The mountains provided wild game and fish with which we supplemented what we raised on the farm. Most of our livelihood came from keeping bees, in partnership with my Grandparents, who lived just across the garden and on the other side of a great shelterbelt of trees. As a child I literally grew up in the proverbial land of milk and honey.

As a North American White male I didn't understand just how much I had been reared in the mind of the oppressor. I was reared with the illusion that we didn't have any problems with racial prejudice in Montana. That was something that happened in the "South," but not here. Negative attitudes toward the Indians or being blind to the suffering the Mexican laborers who worked in the sugar beet fields didn't qualify as racism. Of course, we went to church every Sunday. So I grew up looking at life through rose colored lenses of illusion and denial and it took decades to learn about seeing life through "*The Color Purple.*"

There is much more that could be explored in the wisdom of this remarkable woman, but I want to lift up the incredible insights she shares in her book, *Possessing the Secret of Joy.* This was not an easy book to read because it deals with the deep pain that accompanies the practice of female mutilation. Without the passion she reveals through her primary character, which is the foundation of this story, I would not have persevered to the end of the book in order to discover the *Secret of Joy.* I know of a number of women who said that they had to stop reading the book and return to it later. Some said they never could finish it because it was just too painful.

It seems too easy to reveal the secret of Joy by just naming it. It will not have the impact and deeper significance when separated from the story. However, the secret is revealed in and through political activism and struggle which leads to another crucifixion, which in this case was done at the hands of a firing squad. Yet it reveals a truth that the oppressed and disenfranchised have long known, and which I have only learned from them in recent years.

The secret to possessing Joy is...*Resistance.*

Alice Walker is the incarnation of the Politics of Liberation and Freedom. Thank God this woman found her voice. There are many voices like hers, which get drowned out by the Powers and cultural prejudices that never cease from promoting the Politics of Power and Domination.

Joy is not another synonym for happiness, delight, enjoyment, ecstasy, elation, thrill or bliss as may be listed in the Thesaurus. Most of the songs in the hymnals of my Church fall short of the true meaning of joy. Theology based on the hope of salvation robs people of this deeper meaning of joy by helping them to escape rather than engage in the struggle.

Theology based on the Biblical theme of liberation offers the opportunity to possess "*Joy*" because it offers a model for *resistance*:

- *Joy* is that deep knowing in one's soul that no one can take away your power.

- *Joy* is knowing that you are free.

- *Joy* is knowing that there is hope.

- *Joy* is knowing that love casts out fear.

- *Joy* is the source of courage.
- *Joy* is escaping the mind of the oppressor.
- *Joy* is not a feeling; it is a condition of the soul.

Alice Walker is one of *el pueblo* who found her voice. She shares her Credo and it speaks volumes to those who want to hear.

11

Credo to Credo: John Swomley and I

When I joined the faculty of Saint Paul School of Theology as a full time professor in 1970, Dr. John Swomley had already been teaching there for most of a decade in the area of Social Ethics. He was a peace activist and a pacifist. In reality, at that time, I was neither. While I might have qualified as a person on the liberal side of social concerns, no one would have labeled me as being radical about the struggle for justice.

That same year Swomley published a book entitled, *American Empire: The Political Ethics of 20th Century Conquest.* This was the first time I remember being exposed to the idea that the policies of the United States were largely formed around the notion of "Empire." I learned a great deal more about the American Empire when I went to Nicaragua. Sadly, Swomley's book is still relevant.

Two years later Swomley published another book entitled *Liberation Ethics.* It is a magnificent contribution to understanding the morality and ethics involved in the struggle for liberation. However, in all truthfulness, at the time it was published I wasn't able to grasp the importance of the concepts he set forth. I didn't see how *Liberation Ethics* related to my life. As I look back on that time I probably felt that I wasn't among those who needed to be liberated.

John Swomley was constantly being accused of being a "Communist" for the positions he took, especially as they related to the war in Vietnam. Not only was I not ready to hear what he had to say, I was not ready to risk the constant attacks which were leveled at him from some of the leaders of the Church as well as from the society at large. I do remember that he endured the harassment with grace. He knew how to love the enemy.

In *Liberation Ethics* Swomley says that many people think of liberation as a secular term with chiefly political overtones and redemption as a distinctively religious or theological word. Redemption, however, was at one time a word with no more religious significance than the term *liberation* implies today. Swomley often includes Jesus, Gandhi and Martin Luther King, Jr. in the same sentence to lend emphasis to the idea that there is a cost involved when one engages in the struggle for liberation.

The disciples would have been clear about the cost involved when Jesus invited them to "take up your cross." Jesus was not speaking about a concept of religious redemption. He saw everyone as having a part in the cost of achieving his or her own liberation and not about some redemptive plan where he paid the price and no one else need take any risk in achieving their own freedom. Jesus' endeavor was not about setting people free from sin. Rather, Jesus was about inviting people to be full participants in achieving their own freedom from oppression and doing it in such a way that justice would prevail.

Another emphasis Swomley presents is that liberation is primarily a struggle with systemic evil. It is not about identifying one evil person and eliminating that person. He says that everyone is born into oppressive systems like racism or sexism and that they tend to fit into the system and accept the myths which support or rationalize it. This is what Paulo Freire refers to as the mind of the oppressor. Swomley is quick to say that concentration on changing systems does not mean that individual persons are less important.

Swomley makes the point that most oppressed groups have a limited understanding of the systems that hold them down. They may even accept the system while seeing some need for change within it. For instance, the military or war system may be seen as necessary even when it is clearly an expression of dominance and violence.

Swomley examines how Liberation Ethics relates to violence and reviews a number of historic attempts at liberation in Cuba and Latin America. He reviews different strategies of liberation and reminds the reader that the struggle against oppression is a continuing one. This long view of the struggle means that something extraordinary is required of those who want to be free and who also want others to be free.

I remember a time when I was returning from a conference with Dr. Don Holter, who at that time was the President of Saint Paul School of Theology. He reported a conversation he had just concluded with the Bishop of the Kansas Area of the United Methodist Church. The Bishop told Dr. Holter that a very powerful lay member of the United Methodist Church in Kansas was putting pressure on him to have John Swomley removed from the faculty of the seminary. The primary reason for this action in the eyes of this rich and powerful layperson was that John was a "Communist."

President Holter told the Bishop that he would be more than glad to fire John Swomley if any person could present proof that John had taken any positions that were not in keeping with the Wesleyan Tradition and the Theological Task, which is based on the Bible, Tradition, Experience and Reason. Just to be accused of being Communist without proof, wasn't good enough As far as I know the Bishop never mentioned it again. John Swomley was never fired. The continued presence of John Swomley on the faculty didn't make public relations and fund raising any easier for the president of the seminary.

My Credo has benefited from reading authors such as John Swomley who do their theological homework before speaking their truth to power. While I may not always understand or agree with Swomley, I do know that he is a man of integrity. John is a great model for what it means to be a political activist.

There is no retirement from the struggle when one engages in the Politics of Liberation and Freedom. At the time of this writing Swomley is 91 years old and although he has not taught in the classroom for many years he has never retired. He continues to do research and exercises his freedom to speak the truth to power.

Thanks John.

12

Credo to Credo: Charles Page and I

Dr. Charles Page, a highly respected Christian archeologist from the Jerusalem Center in Israel, was in Montana to present a three-day seminar in March of 2003. The seminar was designed to take us on an archeological journey through the events of Holy Week beginning with Palm Sunday and ending with Easter. I had been to the Holy Land in 1989. By attending this seminar I thought I may have a second chance to "walk where Jesus had walked," and do some further reflection on Jesus and his mission.

We began to look at the activities which occurred on Palm Sunday. Through the use of a power-point slide presentation we could almost feel the event. Page made the political nature of the Palm Sunday event absolutely clear. Jesus was challenging the authorities of his own nation. Charles also believed that Pontius Pilate, the Roman Governor, would have observed the activities of Jesus from his residence across the valley. The challenge to the Powers was brought to a climax when Jesus overturned the tables of the moneychangers in the Temple courtyard.

The next morning I had a brief opportunity to speak with Dr. Page before the session began. I expressed my appreciation for the political importance he attached to the events of Palm Sunday. I was really looking forward to the rest of his presentation on Holy Week.

We were given a clear archeological perspective on the layout of the Temple and the various entrances and courtyards. Page felt that when Jesus was teaching at the Temple during that week he had positioned himself to speak with the people who were disenfranchised. Before Jesus went to Jerusalem the religious authorities, the Chief Priests and Scribes, wanted to find a way to kill him. Now he was really stirring up trouble by speaking truth to power. At the same time, the message Jesus shared was reaching the hearts and minds of *el pueblo*.

Page reviewed what he believed to be the setting for the Last Supper. We followed Jesus to the Garden of Gethsemane prior to his arrest. After Jesus was arrested Page began to focus on the agony of the cross and the pain Jesus must have endured. As he moved on to the Easter narratives it was apparent that he believed that Jesus was the Son of God who had paid the price to reconcile humankind to God.

The third and last morning of the seminar Charles Page reported that a few persons at the seminar had asked him if he really believed that Jesus was the Messiah. When he responded by saying that he did *not* believe that Jesus was the Messiah a kind of shock settled over the group. There was a long pause before he began to speak again. Page reiterated that he did not believe that Jesus was the Messiah, but, went on to say he believed that Jesus would be the Messiah when he returned again and fulfilled the prophecy of the Second Coming. Again there was a moment of silence, but this time it was more like a sigh of relief from the group. The group was comfortably back in the realm of a serious discussion of an orthodox understanding of Christianity.

While Dr. Page introduced some political meaning related to the events of Palm Sunday, he was still being true to a more dominant religious perspective based on the notion that Jesus was primarily going through the motions of fulfilling a previously prophesied role when riding into Jerusalem on the colt of an ass. I guess it would also have been his opinion that Pilate was also simply playing out his part in the script God had predestined.

The conclusion that Jesus would be the Messiah when he returns again takes away the imperative for political action. This approach makes the events of Holy Week fit neatly into the Western mold of religious activities and it keeps the believer looking at the future for the true understanding of God's intention for humankind.

When we escape into the future there is a tendency to lose touch with reality. Engaging in the Politics of Liberation and Freedom is an invitation to engage the issues which life presents to us by staying in the present. Indeed, to be truly alive a person must be in the present. It follows that to be truly political it is essential to live in the present. Being in the present is necessary in order to address reality and not to be distracted by illusion.

The way we view the meaning of time in the Western world influences how we approach reality. Most of us were brought up with a linear view of time which is conceptualized by:

- seeing the *Past* as being behind us;

- perceiving the *Present* as being a fleeting moment in the continuum;

- and viewing the *Future* as being in front of us.

Therefore the past is nothing more than a distortion in our memory, like remembering the good old days, that never actually happened. The future is not much more than an illusion. It is a nice escape because no one requires us to prove that our imagination will stand the test of time.

The concept of time from the Hebrew perspective in which Jesus had his vision shaped had an entirely different model:

- the *Past* is in front of us,

- we are in the creative moment of the *Present* and

- the *Future* is behind us.

I know this may sound very strange at first, but think about it. We look out at what is in front of us and we can see what has already happened. The past is right there in our face. We observe the past and can do some reality testing about what we have accomplished or done to this point in the time continuum.

The future is behind us. We have not yet put our creative or destructive touch on the reality we see. The future will become the past. By a careful examination of the past, which is now in front of us, we will be better able to see what we are doing in the creative moment we call the present. This doesn't take away the use of our imagination but it does test it every day.

This Hebrew perspective requires a great deal more responsibility and allows for less escape. We are engaged in the process of creation as subjects rather than the objects of creation. The Biblical theme of liberation captures this understanding when it offers the challenge to construct a just society now and not wait for some future bliss in heaven. It means we have to engage in systemic change and not submit to the structures of domination. This Hebrew view of time views God as involved in the creative process and also as fully engaged in the struggle for justice. We can see the injustice, which is simply a view of what we have accomplished or failed to accomplish up to this point in time. We can, with the participation of God, address the injustice so that what emerges as a result of our endeavors in the present results in more a more just society.

There is a story about three men who were together in New York City when the news came that within thirty minutes a huge tidal wave would engulf the city and there was no time to escape the impending disaster. One of these men was an atheist and said he was heading to the nearest bar to get drunk because there wasn't much time left to be with his friends. The second man was a "Christian" and said he was headed for the nearest church to pray for the salvation of his soul. The third man was in touch with his Hebrew heritage and offered the opinion that they had just thirty minutes to learn how to breathe under water.

Charles Page, a committed Christian archeologist, has reminded me that it is the past that is in front of me and, there are some serious changes that need to be made. One change to be considered is how we view Jesus and his example in the struggle against oppressive systems.

13

Credo-to-Credo: Marcus Borg and I

It is with great respect that I approach this brief dialogue with Marcus Borg. For many people his scholarship has contributed to a new understanding of the Bible. In his book, *Meeting Jesus Again for the First Time,* he is moved by an awareness of Jesus as a subversive who had a social vision of the Kingdom of God based on compassion.

Marcus and his colleagues in the Jesus Seminar have opened the door to the Bible so it plays a more vital part with our contemporary experience of life. Borg wants people to take the Bible "seriously but not literally." Borg's Credo is expanded in his book, *The Heart of Christianity,* where he offers a way for people to be passionate believers today. He identifies two paradigms that illustrate the differences in approaches to understanding the Bible and in the goals of believers.

In what Borg identifies as the *Earlier Paradigm* the primary emphasis is about an afterlife and what one must believe, or do, to be saved. It is an explanation of what I call Salvation Theology. He says it has been the most common expression of Christianity for the past several hundred years. And he reminds us that it is the most visible form of Christianity in our own day.

Most of Borg's book is intended to introduce and develop what he identifies as the *Emerging Paradigm.* In this paradigm he says the emphasis is the transformation of this life through a relationship with God. This approach to faith is about having a relationship with God which transforms life in the present while affirming religious pluralism. He spells out a convincing case for what it means to be true to the Christian Tradition. He is artful in focusing the dialogue by utilizing the metaphor of "heart" to take us through this emerging paradigm.

In the chapter entitled *The Kingdom of God: The Heart of Justice,* Borg makes a strong case that the Bible is political as well as personal. He seemed to be in accord with the content of my own Credo as he identifies God's passion for justice as a neglected emphasis. He sees how this passion for justice is spelled out in both the Hebrew Bible (Old Testament) and in the New Testament.

I am in harmony with him until he begins to write about the political meaning of the Cross. He makes the case that Good Friday and Easter have a political meaning and that the cross is an indictment of the domination systems. Then, in a brief transition, his assessment of the cross shifts to how this event fits into his emphasis on personal transformation. He says the cross is both personal and political and then goes on to say that the cross embodies the path of personal transformation, "of being born again by dying and rising with Christ." It is at this point that I have the sense that he begins to pull his political punches.

By using these metaphors of dying and rising with Christ, which were at the heart of Paul's Christology, Borg leaves the political struggle and returns to the matter of religious persuasion. He is apparently trying to avoid the pitfalls of the atonement theory according to which Christ paid the price for our sins. However, he promotes the idea that this event carries with it the inspiration for transformation into a more meaningful spiritual life, which strikes me as nothing more than another atonement theory.

Borg reviews the need for some consciousness-raising in the Church and encourages advocacy of God's justice. He doesn't have a name for this kind of participation in the political process but offers a few possibilities such as, "progressive politics," "a politics of compassion," or "the politics of the Kingdom." However, this is viewed as only "a political dimension" of the Christian and not at the heart of Christian life.

I am encouraged by the genuine courage Marcus Borg expresses in his Credo. In the chapter on the *Heart of Justice* he speaks truth to power. He has lined up with the author of the book of James in the New Testament, by making a case that faith without works is dead. He wants to keep our spiritual life in balance: giving our attention to God and also while giving some of our energy to compassion and justice in this life.

Borg says that Christians in our time are called to be political and then lets us off the hook by saying this does not mean that we are all called to be political activists. Once again he defers to the writing attributed to Paul, who says we all have different gifts and then proceeds to list them. Being a political activist was not on Paul's list and it should have been because Jesus said that if you would follow him then it means that you will need to "take up your cross." We should remember that it was Paul who took the imperative for insurrection out of the process by focusing on the religious doctrines of salvation. For Paul, the political struggle for justice is secondary. I can't help feeling that this is where Borg ends up as well.

I appreciate the insights Borg presents on how to read the Scripture and engage in a life of faith, but at the same time he finally stays in the realm of religion. He concludes his book by expressing his belief that there are several paths to God. He wants us to learn to get along and respect each other with the added encouragement that we can, in our own way, find our way up the mountain to God.

In contrast I believe the message of the Gospels is that we don't need to climb a mountain to find God. Rather, God comes down from the mountain to walk with us. Jesus' model for political action, The Politics of Liberation and Freedom, is firmly based on the understanding that God is a full participant in the struggle for justice.

In the final analysis the paradigm Marcus Borg offers about the emerging shape of Christianity and the nature of the Christian church does not truly represent a serious challenge the Powers and governing authorities of our day. Jesus' purpose in going to the cross went beyond the need for transforming individual lives. He gave his life as a model about how to challenge and transform oppressive systems. The struggle goes on. After all, *el pueblo* are still with us. Indeed, if we are truly honest about it, our own freedom is at stake.

I would invite Marcus Borg to meet Jesus one more time. The "*heart*", or central focus, of Jesus life is not about personal transformation; it is about social liberation. Adopting the method of non-violent *agape* is precisely how we can be passionate believers today.

14

Credo to Credo: Alvin and Heidi Toffler and I

In their book, *Creating A New Civilization: The Politics of the Third Wave*, Alvin and Heidi Toffler, say that America faces a convergence of crises unmatched since its earliest days. Its family system is in crisis, but so is its health system, its urban systems and *above all its political system, which for all practical purposes has lost the confidence of the people.* (Emphasis is mine)

The Tofflers have been sharing their analysis and vision for change since 1970. The promotional material for this book says their works have been read by presidents, Prime Ministers, CEO's and students. In other words, their futurist analysis has been widely read by those we refer to in this book as the Powers. Their writings are less well known by the general public and certainly *el pueblo* have not had much chance to be introduced to the concepts shared by the Tofflers.

A brief quote from Chapter One, entitled, *"SUPER STRUGGLE,"* will give you a glimpse of what they are inviting us to consider:

> "A new civilization is emerging in our lives, and blind men everywhere are trying to suppress it. This new civilization brings with it new family styles, changed ways of working, loving, and living, a new economy, new political conflicts, and beyond all of this an altered consciousness as well.
>
> "Until now the human race has undergone two great waves of change, each one largely obliterating earlier cultures of civilization and replacing them with ways of life inconceivable to those who came before. The First Wave of change—the agricultural revolution—took thousands of years to play itself out. The Second Wave—the rise of industrial civilization—took a mere three hundred years. Today history is even more accelerative, and it is likely that the Third Wave will sweep across history and complete itself in a few decades. Those of us who happen to share the planet at this explosive moment will therefore feel the full impact of the Third Wave in our own lifetimes.

"This new civilization has its own distinctive world outlook; its own way of dealing with time; space, logic and causality. And its own principles for the politics of the future."

The changes envisioned by the Tofflers are really happening. All of us recognize that technology is increasing the speed of change and in spite of the benefits, we often find ourselves resisting the change. Their concern is that many people, including those in positions of power, want to retain traditional values as though they are cut in tablets of stone. I have been referring to many of these traditions and values as the mind of the oppressor. The Tofflers want to see them changed. So do I. I wonder if we are speaking of the same thing.

Along with the Tofflers there are other creative thinkers who want to make sense of the conflict and chaos we are currently living through. There has been an ongoing search for paradigms around which to organize the new civilization. Some scholars in addressing the rapid rate of change say the old myths are passing away and new myths by which we are going to live have not yet emerged.

Most people would agree that many of the traditional foundations on which we depended are crumbling. Therefore it is more important than ever to work on our Credos so we can know where we stand, and have a solid place to begin our efforts at re-visioning.

I have great appreciation for the analysis of the Tofflers. To ignore their vision is to join the "blind men" who are trying to suppress the change. The Church is one of the main systems that resists change and does so with a vengeance. In the midst of the insecurity that this monumental cultural shift introduces, it seems that the only thing the Christian Church has to offer is the security blanket of Salvation Theology.

In the search for new paradigms I think it is worth re-visiting an old paradigm which can make a contribution in the shaping of the new civilization. Rather than seeing Jesus as a relic of an old First Wave civilization, I am convinced that he has provided us with a political model upon which we can build a more just future, i.e., the Politics of Liberation and Freedom.

If we want to engage in the "SUPER STRUGGLE" as expressed by the Tofflers we must be full participants in addressing the crisis in the political systems which dominate our lives. The political model Jesus offered can be just as relevant today as it was when Jesus lived, maybe more relevant. The Tofflers would support my suggestion that every person must be a political activist in the process or end up as another casualty of the current crisis.

The Tofflers say that some generations are born to create. They believe that we are participating in just such an historical moment. They believe that in every sphere of social life (in our families, our schools, our businesses, our church, our energy systems and communications), we face an urgent need to create new forms. They emphasize that nowhere is obsolescence more dangerous than in our political life. They say that in no other field today do we find less imagination, less experimentation, less willingness to contemplate fundamental change. Perhaps they should look once again at the church systems that seem to be competing in exhibit the greatest refusal to accept to the new reality.

The Tofflers believe that resistance to the changes occurring in the Third Wave will escalate the possibility of violence and our own destruction. In the time that has passed since they wrote this book, the violence has escalated beyond that which even they might have dared to imagine. The violence of 9/11 and initiation of a preemptive war in Iraq only underline the Tofflers prophetic vision. Our own national territory has now become part of the war zone and fear abounds.

When I say that Jesus invites us to engage in the Politics of Liberation and Freedom, he is not inviting us to express more resistance to change, not at all. He is inviting us to challenge the injustice the Powers defend as part of the tradition because it benefits them to do so. It is through non-violent *agape* and political activism that the future must be molded.

Ostensibly the Tofflers have not engaged in any theological discourse in their books. To read their writings as though they are not expressing theories that have theological significance is to continue to wear blinders. We must remove the scales from our eyes that separate theology and politics if we are to understand that creation of a new civilization is not simply in the hands of politicians, economists and social scientists. When we speak of creation we are speaking of theology at the same time. The very traditions that have kept politics and religion separated must be part of what is restructured.

I believe the Tofflers are very serious about wanting to contribute to a more humane civilization. They concur with me in recognizing that the institutional Church is one of the social systems that need to change, especially as it continues to support the camp of Second Wave politics.

I am concerned however that the Tofflers are primarily addressing their concerns to the Powers themselves who move in the halls of government and corporate influence. I don't feel that they have considered how to participate with *el pueblo*, especially those who are exploited by the new forms of globalization and neo-liberalism. For instance, the Tofflers regard those who stood in opposition to the North American Free Trade Agreement (NAFTA) as those who are blind and resisting the Third Wave economy. If NAFTA and CAFTA (Central American Free Trade Agreement) are the wave of the future then there is much more work that needs to be done to attend to the needs of *el pueblo*.

The Tofflers make the point that the Third Wave forces in America have yet to find their voice and the political party that gives it to them will *dominate* the American future. This approach to politics has the appearance of the Politics of Power and Domination with a poorly disguised makeover.

A major emphasis in their analysis is to keep the United States from being left behind and losing our competitive edge in the world of business and trade. In their book there is an entire chapter given to "*The Way We Make Wealth*." The Tofflers identify ten features of the Third Wave economy that identify monumental changes in how wealth is created. They say that the conversion of the United States, Japan and Europe to this new system, though not complete, represents the single most important change in the global economy since the industrial revolution.

We should consider the wisdom of a First Wave indigenous politician named Jesus who said "you cannot serve both God and Mammon (wealth)." We should be seeking conversion from the mind of the oppressor instead of figuring out ways to maintain our own nation in a position of dominance, privilege and wealth.

For those who believe in the Second Coming of Jesus, now would be a good time to re-evaluate. Belief in the second coming does not relieve us of the responsibility to contribute to the development of the new technological civilization. Since Jesus has not returned again as soon as the Apostle Paul expected, and for all we know, may never return; I recommend that we join in the re-insurrection and join in the Politics of Liberation and Freedom. The message of the Tofflers is that change is occurring so fast that we may have already been left behind.

I would add a word of thanks to the Tofflers for the depth of their analysis. We all must learn about what they have already learned in their research if we want to engage in the "SUPER STRUGGLE." To the Tofflers I would also offer the same invitation John Wesley made to folks with whom he might have had some doctrinal conflict when he said, "If your heart is with my heart…give me your hand." Let's go forward together to build that more humane civilization you envision and which, Jesus refers to as the Kingdom of God.

15

Credo to Credo: Diana Eck and I

Freedom of religion is a political concept that has a central role in the ongoing development of democracy in the United States. The challenge this represents is set forth with forceful clarity in Diana Eck's recently published book, *A New Religious America: How a "Christian Country" Has Become the World's Most Religiously Diverse Nation.*

Eck says that we must embrace the religious diversity that comes with our commitment to religious freedom. She says that it will require the engagement of our religious traditions in the common tasks of our civil society. I couldn't agree more. What she calls "common tasks of our civil society" I call "political action."

I have been suggesting that a person's Credo is a key to dialogue at every level of life, including but not limited to the area of religious expression. Eck broadens this when she says that articulating one's own faith anew in a world of many faiths is a task for people of every religious tradition today. To be able to sustain meaningful communication across religious and political differences we must be clear about our own personal Credo and be able to respect the Credo of others.

The Politics of Liberation and Freedom is a natural fit with Eck's vision of finding a model for a truly pluralistic, multi-religious society. Both focus on promoting justice for all who share in our civil society. Both require a commitment to the respect the sovereignty of the individual.

Diana Eck and I are from the same home town of Bozeman, Montana. Although we are separated by a generation of time we both had our earliest spiritual formation in the Bozeman United Methodist Church before we ventured beyond Bozeman. The discovery of other religions and cultures has been an important part of shaping each of our lives and Credos. An earlier period of Eck's spiritual journey is expressed in her book *Encountering God: A Spiritual Journey from Bozeman to Banaras* for which she was awarded the prestigious Grawemeyer Book Award. She affirms that her own faith was not threatened, but broadened and deepened by the study of Hindu, Buddhist, Muslim and Sikh traditions of faith.

Eck is very clear in her conclusion that whether we recognize it or not, each of us as individuals and all of us as a community are caught up in the diversity and that the shaping of the new religious America is an unfinished story with both national and global implications.

One of the hymns that has been sung down through the generations of the United Methodist Church is entitled, *Open My Eyes, That I May See*. This is a "prayer hymn" which seems appropriate to share at this point. As follows:

> Open my *eyes*, that I may see glimpses of truth thou hast for me;
>   Place in my hands the wonderful key that shall unclasp and set me free.
> Silently now I wait for thee, Ready, my God thy will to see,
>   Open my *eyes* illumine me, Spirit divine!
> Open my *ears*, that I may hear voices of truth thou sendest clear;
>   And while the wave notes fall on my ear, everything false will disappear.
> Silently now I wait for thee, Ready, my God thy will to see;
>   Open my *ears*, illumine me, Spirit divine.
> Open my *mouth*, and let me bear gladly the warm truth everywhere;
>   Open my *heart* and let me prepare love with thy children thus to share.
> Silently now I wait for thee, Ready, my God thy will to see;
>   Open my *heart*, illumine me, Spirit divine!

> Clara H. Scott, 1841–1897

Traditions of Christian dominance and exclusivism only lead to more violence, both here in the United States and around the world. I heartily join those who find hope in this eye-opening account of the changing political and religious landscape of America.

16

Credo to Credo: Nelson Mandela and I

Non-violent *agape* is the methodology for political action that Jesus lived and taught. Sadly, most people, including an overwhelming majority of those who declare their belief in him as the Son of God and Messiah, continue to reject non-violence as a viable means to address the struggle for liberation and freedom.

In his autobiography, *Long Walk to Freedom*, Nelson Mandela reviews the historic political struggle in South Africa. The political and social changes that have occurred in South Africa provide convincing evidence that challenging the Powers through non-violence is a sound, albeit not an easy, approach to the struggle. It is hard to find a more profound illustration to show that refusing to cooperate with social, legal, and economic violence can actually result in genuine liberation for both the oppressed and the oppressor.

Nelson Mandela and the other leaders of the African National Congress have always acknowledged their debt to Gandhi. They shaped their own approach to achieving liberation on Gandhi's twenty-one years of struggle against racial and economic prejudice in South Africa before he returned to India and took up the struggle for liberation and freedom in his homeland. In his autobiography Gandhi said,

> "I can say with assurance, as a result of all my experiments, that a perfect vision of Truth can only follow a complete realization of Ahimsa (non-violence). To see the universal and all-pervading Spirit of Truth face-to-face, one must be able to love the meanest of creation as oneself. And a man who aspires after that cannot afford to keep out of any field of life.
>
> "That is why my devotion to Truth has drawn me into the field of politics; and I can say without the slightest hesitation, and yet in all humility, that those who say that religion has nothing to do with politics do not know what religion means. And...all this is passing before our very eyes, but there are none so blind as those who will not see."

It is also worth recalling other teaching Gandhi shared with the world:

Gandhi's Eleven Vows

1. Non-violence in thought, speech and action.
2. Truth in thought, speech and action.
3. Non-stealing.
4. Pursuing the ultimate, devoid of passion. (Chastity)
5. Non-possession.
6. To respect and practice manual labor.
7. Control of the palate. (Eat to live and not for taste; and live for service to humanity.)
8. To become fearless in all respects.
9. To give equal respect to all religions.
10. Love of neighbor.
11. To treat everybody as an equal human being.

Gandhi's Seven Sins

1. Wealth without work.
2. Pleasure without conscience.
3. Knowledge without character.
4. Commerce without morality.
5. Science without humanity.
6. Worship without sacrifice.
7. Politics without principle.

Nelson Mandela became a key figure in the political insurrection of oppressed people in South Africa. In public settings, in court, and especially from his prison cell, Mandela spoke truth to power by speaking truth to his people. Ordinary men and women chose to follow his lead and manifest forgiveness in the face of cruel and unremitting violence. It was an amazing struggle that even changed the hearts and minds of their enemies. The integrity of the movement reached beyond South Africa and raised consciousness around the globe. It is a contemporary illustration of forgiving seven times seventy.

The struggle in South Africa was truly "a long walk to freedom." Over half of the last century was required to validate non-violence as a legitimate approach to achieve human rights and civil liberties. In an address to the African National Congress Youth League, in December of 1951, Nelson Mandela spoke in a way that is amazingly relevant today:

"Mankind as a whole is today standing on the threshold of great events—events that at times seem to threaten its very existence. On the one hand, there are those groups, parties, or persons that are prepared to go to war in defence of colonialism, imperialism, and their profits. These groups, at the head of which stand the ruling circles in America, are determined to perpetuate a permanent atmosphere of crisis and fear in the world. Knowing that a frightened world cannot think clearly, these groups attempt to create conditions under which the common men might be inveigled into supporting the building of more and more atomic bombs, bacteriological weapons and other instruments of mass destruction.

"These crazy men whose prototype is to be found at the head of the trusts and cartels of America and Western Europe do not realise that they will suffer the destruction that they are contemplating for their innocent fellow beings. But they are desperate and become more so as they realise the determination of the common men to preserve peace.

"Yes, the common man who for generations has been the tool of insane politicians and governments, who has suffered privations and sorrow in wars that were of profit to tiny privileged groups, is today rising from being the object of history to becoming the subject of history. For the ordinary men and women in the world, the oppressed all over the world are becoming the conscious creators of their own history. They are pledged to carve their destiny and not to leave it in the hands of tiny ruling circles—or classes.

"Whilst the dark and sinister forces in the world are organizing a desperate and last-minute fight to defend a decadent and bankrupt civilisation, the common people, full of confidence and buoyant hope, struggle for the creation of a new, united, and prosperous human family..."

The *Long Walk to Freedom* required a long view of the struggle. Engaging in systemic change is an endeavor that calls for lots of courage, lots of patience and lots of forgiveness. Currently, interventions from structures of corporate globalism and the so-called New World Order continue to impact the internal struggle for life and dignity in South Africa, especially in the area of economic opportunity.

Living with economic, racial, and religious diversity is no easy task. Affirming diversity is not about setting aside differences. It is rather about embracing differences. One of the important aspects revealed in this story of the political struggle is how the different religious groups and churches in South Africa set aside their doctrinal and cultural differences in order to focus their love and energy on the more vital and urgent matters of freedom and justice. Not only did religious leaders support the morality of the struggle, but many paid a price for their political activism by being jailed or martyred.

In his speech, Mandela said that the common man was engaged in the struggle for the "creation of a new, united and prosperous human family." I couldn't help but think of an event in life of Jesus that was recorded in the three New Testament Gospels of Mark, Matthew, and Luke. The situation in this brief cameo was that Jesus had challenged the *Powers* to the point that his family was alarmed and concerned for his well being. Indeed, they felt he was in such serious danger that they went together in order to bring Jesus home.

> "Then his mother and his brothers came; and standing outside, they sent to him and called him. A crowd was sitting around him; and they said to Jesus, 'Your mother and your brothers and sisters are outside, asking for you.' And he replied, 'Who are my mother and my brothers?' And looking at those who sat around him, he said, 'Here are my mother and my brothers! Whoever does the will of God is my brother and sister and mother.'" (Mark 3)

The current political/religious mantra regarding "family values" in the United States totally misses the mark. This political mantra which is supposedly informed by traditional Christian values resists and ignores the way Jesus elevates "family values" to a level higher than racial or family blood lines. Jesus vision of "family" even takes us beyond blind national patriotism. The understanding of "family" Jesus introduces promotes a vision of political activism designed to break down the walls of hostility which divide the human family. Jesus revealed a God whose "will" is to create a society with justice for all. As such, the Politics of Liberation and Freedom is an approach to the struggle which includes a global vision for freedom and justice.

Nelson Mandela and the people of South Africa are still promoting a global vision for freedom and justice. Indeed, *el pueblo* in Nicaragua are still struggling to create "a new man and a new society" which also includes a global vision for freedom and justice. It is their common struggle for justice that unites *el pueblo* on opposite sides of the globe.

Nelson Mandela has become a living legend. I am very concerned that the story of South Africa is becoming obscured and lost. We must not let that happen because there is no doubt in my mind that Jesus would include Nelson Mandela in his vision of "family."

Thank you my Brother!

17

Conclusion

Jesus said, "Enter through the narrow gate: for the gate is wide and the road is easy that leads to destruction, and there are many who take it. For the gate is narrow and the road is hard that leads to life, and there are few who find it."

Jesus recognized that cooperation with the Powers and domination systems is the easy road that leads to destruction. He challenged the Politics of Power and Domination and the delusion that you can achieve peace and justice through violence. Jesus offered a genuine alternative that is still relevant today.

Jesus invites us to participate in the *Politics of Liberation and Freedom*.

Jesus invites us to embrace a *Theology of Grace*.

Jesus invites us to adopt a *Methodology of Non-Violent Love*.

The Biblical Theme of liberation does not offer an easy walk to freedom. To engage in the struggle for justice takes more courage and more faith, so it is important to remember that we are not alone. God is with us!

The *Good News* is that there are some who find *The Narrow Gate*!

This is my Credo.

Epilogue

Originally I thought I might be in Nicaragua for just a few years. By 1996 I had been there for most of twelve years. I had been blessed by opportunities to be a part of projects initiated and administered by the Nicaraguan people.

Many citizens from the United States had come to Nicaragua. Participants often asked their Nicaraguan hosts what they might do to be helpful. Over and over again I heard the same response, "Go home and change the policies of your own government."

In 1996, I decided that it was time to return to the United States. The culture in the United States had changed during the years I was away. I had also changed and while I might be returning to live "*in*" this culture, I was no longer "*of*" this culture.

My goal to change U.S. foreign policy came into focus as I joined the project to close the U.S. Army School of the Americas (S.O.A.) located at Ft. Benning, Georgia. The list of atrocities that the graduates of this military training school have committed in Latin America over the last half-century is well documented. Just a few examples of the violence perpetrated by the military trained at the School of the Americas include:

- During the Somoza dictatorship, officers of the Nicaraguan National Guard trained at the S.O.A. were guilty of torture, murder and other human rights violations against their own people. After the fall of Somoza, many of these military officers, became the core leaders for the Contras, which were sponsored and trained by the C.I.A..

- The man who assassinated Bishop Romero in El Salvador in 1980 was trained at the S.O.A..

- Those responsible for the murder of four U. S. church workers and nuns in El Salvador were graduates.

- The troops who were responsible for the massacre of the entire village of El Mozote in El Salvador (800 people), were trained at the S.O.A..

- In 1989 those who carried out the assassination of six Jesuit Priests, their housekeeper and her daughter at the University of Central America in San Salvador were trained at the S.O.A..

In 2001 the U. S. House of Representatives made an attempt to deflect public criticism by changing the name of the S.O.A. to, the Western Hemisphere Institute for Security Cooperation. In Latin America it is still known as the *School of Assassins.* At the annual demonstration in 2005, there were about 20,000 concerned citizens who showed up to express their opposition through non-violent protest. More people were arrested and more time spent in jail. These annual demonstrations are basically ignored by the news media, but the struggle continues.

By December of 1998 I had moved back to my hometown of Bozeman, Montana. Since that time I have continued working to close the U.S. Army School of the Americas, worked as a driver for the Gallatin Valley Food Bank; developed a free counseling service called the "Listening Circle," participated with peace and justice groups, and served as the pastor of the Blackfeet United Methodist Parish located next to Glacier National Park from 2002–2004

My life theme, mentioned earlier in this book, has changed somewhat:

> *Poverty:* The *context* of the struggle for freedom, including my own spiritual poverty.

> *Peace:* The *goal* of the struggle. There is no genuine peace without justice. Inner peace, comes from joining in the politics of liberation and freedom.

> *Love:* Non-violent *agape* is the *method* for the struggle, including love for one's self.

Glossary of Terms

Agape:
>God's kind of love. In this book it refers to the kind of fervent good will and burning passion needed to achieve true freedom and address injustice and evil in all of their various forms.

Bible:
>A reference to the Sacred Scriptures of the Christian tradition which generally includes the Old and New Testaments as adopted in the 4th Century A.D.

Campesino/a:
>In Spanish the word "campo" means the countryside or fields. A campesino/a is a man or woman from the countryside. In our U.S. idiom they are called peasants.

Christian Base Communities, CEB:
>"Base," as it is used here, refers to the people who live at the bottom of the socio/economic pyramid. While there may be some participants who are well off, the participants are essentially made up of the poor. These small groups, i.e., Christian Communities, gather to read and reflect on political and social reality in the light of the Gospel. Through "praxis," action-reflection, they determine what they must do to address injustice and bring about the reign of God on this earth. These groups are the source of Liberation Theology, i.e., a belief in a God who participates in the struggle for peace and justice. Although the number of people who participate in these groups are a small percentage of the population they represent a challenge to the authorities of the church as well as the Powers and domination systems.

Christology:
>This is in reference to how we express our understanding of how Jesus came to be known as the Messiah or Christ. When a person says they are a

Christian they have adopted a belief in Christ. The content of that belief is their Christology.

Church:

The institutional forms, structures, customs and rituals of the Christian Religion which have developed over the centuries since Jesus lived; the Christian Church as a whole.

Credo:

A statement of belief made by an individual or assemblage of people; generally any creed or stated position related to a theological concept; the basis of belief from which a person enters into dialogue with others.

Experience:

With regard to the theological task in the Wesleyan Tradition, experience may relate to both secular or religious experiences that help shape a person's understanding of life and reality.

Freedom:

Having civil liberty and the right to exercise one's free will in the pursuit of justice; to be free from oppression, threats or violence.

God:

A general concept used in reference to an infinite or supreme being. In the Judeo-Christian tradition the creator of the world with whom humanity relates through prayer, worship and moral living. (see Chapter 11 on the Trinity)

Insurrection:

A political uprising which challenges the authority of established systems of control held over people by civil government and/or occupation by a foreign power.

Just War Theory: (As it relates to Christian Tradition)
1. The war must have a *just cause.*
2. It must be waged by a *legitimate authority.*
3. It must be *formally declared.*
4. It must be fought with a *peaceful intention.*
5. It must be a *last resort.*
6. There must be a reasonable *hope of success.*

7. The means used must possess *proportionality* to the end sought.

Three additional conditions must be met regarding conduct permissible during warfare:
1. *Noncombatants* must be given immunity.
2. *Prisoners* must be treated humanely.
3. *International treaties* and *conventions* must be honored.

Kingdom of God:
> The political domain or earthly state in which peace with justice prevails under the sovereignty of God.

Kingdom of Heaven:
> A faith based concept of a place where God reigns eternally; a place of existence where life continues beyond mortal death; a place of justice and bliss which is the prototype for the Kingdom of God on earth.

Liberation:
> To be set free from a situation of oppression or persecution.

La Insurrección Evangelica—The Gospel Insurrection:
> A program developed in the 1980's by the Christian Base Communities in Nicaragua to engage in the struggle for their national independence through the practice of non-violence.

Messiah:
> Messiah is the Hebrew word for the hoped for savior or liberator of the Jewish Tradition. In the Christian tradition Jesus is seen as having fulfilled this prophetic role. It is synonymous with the word Christ which comes from the Greek language.

Methodology:
> General set of principles or actions taken to accomplishing the goals of an individual or group.

Paradigm:
> A pattern, principle, model or archetype around which persons and social groups organize their lives.

Politics:

In this Credo, the meaning of the word, "politics," is about the structuring and ordering of matters of the State and other social systems so that justice is achieved and freedom abounds. Honoring the sovereignty of each person is at the heart of political action. Therefore, the concept of politics must not be limited to or confused with the activities of the Powers and domination systems in their struggle with each other (and with the people) in an attempt to maintain positions of privilege and power.

Politics of Liberation and Freedom:

The political approach Jesus introduced to promote the Kingdom of God and to achieve the freedom of his homeland. This struggle would require a commitment of love, faith and passion in a vigorous and unflagging pursuit of justice as called for by the Old Testament prophets.

Politics of Power and Domination:

The political approach use by Powers and domination systems to maintain their position of authority.

Powers and domination systems:

These words are in reference to nation states, corporations, educational institutions, police, courts, prisons, church hierarchies, etc.; presidents, prime ministers, CEO's, generals, civic authorities, patriarchal and matriarchal heads of families, pastors, and others who impose their will upon others. Through the use of power and violence they may be contributors to injustice which takes the form of racism, sexism, militarism and poverty.

Reason:

With regard to the theological task in the Wesleyan Tradition it refers to the human capacity to present one's beliefs in a manner which seems logical or makes sense to the believer and to those with whom the belief statements are shared. It does not refer to scientific proof of facts or comments.

Sandinista:

The name taken by the participants in the revolution in Nicaragua in the 1970's, in memory of Augusto Sandino. Sandino led an insurrection against the United States Marines who occupied Nicaragua in the early years of the 20th Century.

School of the Americas—S.O.A.:

> The U.S. Army School of the Americas is a military training center where they train military personnel from Latin American countries. The graduates of the S.O.A. have a horrible record of massacres, torture and human rights violations. The name was changed in 2001 to the Western Hemisphere Institute for Security Cooperation but it uses the same campus, curriculum and staff as the S.O.A.. In Latin America it is known as the *School of Assassins*.

State:

> A general reference to a sovereign nation and its political governance.

Systemic Evil:

> Social practices which result in injustice or harm to the society in general and/or to individuals; such as racism, sexism, oppression, political persecution, war and violence.

Theology:

> This word is formed from the combination of two Greek words: *Theos* (God) and *Logos* (Word). It is how we express our understanding of God. For instance to say that God is Love; or that God is the Creator; are illustrative.

Tradition:

> With regard to the theological task in the Wesleyan Tradition, the word "tradition" primarily refers to church history and may include those practices which have become unique to one denomination or another.

Trinity:

> Is in reference to the view that God has revealed God's self to in three ways. In Christian tradition this has been expressed as the Father, Son and Holy Spirit. It may be expressed as: God the creator, Jesus the liberator, and God the Spirit present with us for guidance and for strength. (See Chapter 11, on The Trinity)

Wesleyan Tradition:

> The Theological Task in the Wesleyan Tradition is a methodology composed of four fundamental areas that contribute to how to express one's beliefs: Bible, Tradition, Experience and Reason.

Zealots:

A militant group of Jews who advocated a military overthrow of Roman Rule and threatened other Jews who cooperated with the Romans. They were part of the uprising that led the Roman Empire to destroy Jerusalem and the Temple in the year A.D. 70.

Author Information

George W. Baldwin

Born: Great Falls, Montana on October 16, 1933

Education:

BA University of Washington, Seattle, WA
BD Garrett Graduate School of Theology, Evanston, IL
Fellow in Residence, The Menninger Foundation, Topeka KS
MDiv Dubuque Theological Seminary,
MA & PhD. University of Missouri

Work History:

U.S. Army Officer, 19561958 (three years)
Pastoral Work in Indiana, Montana and Kansas (fourteen years)
Professor at Saint Paul School of Theology (United Methodist) (fourteen years)

Subsequent Experience:

In 1984 I went to Nicaragua to live in voluntary poverty. While there I lived and worked in the village of Paiwas with people who had been displaced by the terrorism of the Contras and participated in developing 12 re-settlement villages; later I worked directly with Christian Base Communities and La Insurrección *Evangelica*. From July 1, 1989 June 30, 1990, I traveled around the world and shared the story of the Church of the Poor (Liberation Theology) based on experience with Christian Base Communities in Nicaragua. After returning to Nicaragua I worked with widows and orphans in La Casa de La Mujer in the village of Paiwas; I also worked with the Nicaragua Center for Human Rights in the Matagalpa region.

In 1992 I helped organize and participated in an Ecumenical Pilgrimage for Peace and Life from Panama City to Washington D.C. (5000 miles) to raise awareness about the 500th Anniversary of the arrival of Christopher Columbus.

In June 1996 I returned from Nicaragua to live in the United States and continue to live in solidarity with those who live in the context of poverty and pursue matters of peace and social justice. (see Epilogue)

My mailing address is: 10 W. Garfield, Bozeman, Montana, 59715

Suggested Reading

Ched Myers,
> *Binding The Strong Man: A Political Reading of Marks's Story of Jesus*, Orbis Books, Maryknoll, NY 1988

Walter Wink,
> *The Powers That Be: Theology for a New Millennium*, Doubleday1998

Robert McAfee Brown,
> *Unexpected News: Reading the Bible with Third World Eyes*, Westminster John Knox Press 1984
> *Saying Yes and Saying No: On Rendering to God and Caesar*, Westminster Press 1986

Jack Nelson-Pallmeyer,
> *Jesus Against Christianity: Reclaiming the Missing Jesus*, Trinity Press International 2001
> *The War Against the Poor: Low-Intensity Conflict and Christian Faith*, Orbis Books 1989

Marcus Borg,
> *The Heart of Christianity: Rediscovering a Life of Faith*, Harper, 2003
> *Reading the Bible Again for The First Time: Taking the Bible Seriously but Not Literally*, Harper, San Francisco, 2001

Robert W. Funk, Roy W. Hoover and The Jesus Seminar,
> *The Five Gospels*, Scribner 1997

Paulo Freire,
> *Pedagogy of the Oppressed*, translated by Myra Bergman Ramos, Continuum, New York 1970

Leonardo Boff,
> *Francis of Assisi: A Model for Human Liberation*, Orbis Books 2006

Alice Walker,
   Possessing the Secret of Joy, Pocket Books 1992

Alvin and Heidi Toffler,
   Creating A New Civilization: The Politics of The Third Wave, Turner 1995

Kader Asmal, David, Wilmot James, Editors:
   Nelson Mandela: In His Own Words, Little, Brown and Company, New York 2003

Diana Eck,
   A NEW RELIGIOUS AMERICA: How a "Christian Country" Has Now Become the World's Most Religiously Diverse Nation, HarperCollins, San Francisco, 2001

Obery M. Hendricks, Jr.
   The Politics of Jesus, Doubleday, New York 2006

978-0-595-41579-3
0-595-41579-2

Printed in the United States
73974LV00004B/148-195

9 780595 415793